When God Made Rest

George E. Vandeman

Pacific Press Publishing Association
Boise, Idaho
Oshawa, Ontario, Canada

Edited by Don Mansell
Designed by Tim Larson
Cover Photo by Nona Guerriere
Type Set in 10/12 Century Schoolbook

Unless otherwise indicated, scripture references in this book
are from the New King James Version.

Library of Congress Catalog Card Number: 87-42713

ISBN 0-8163-0722-9

87 88 89 90 91 ● 5 4 3 2 1

Contents

Fingerprints in Stone	5
When God Made Rest	16
A Day to Remember	24
Since the Day He Died	32
The Mystery of Lawlessness	46
Centuries Tell Their Story	61
When No Man Can Buy or Sell	74
Tyranny of the Crowd	85

Fingerprints
in Stone

The year 1968 was a bitter pill to swallow. January stormed in with the North Korean capture of the U.S.S. *Pueblo* and the shocking Tet Offensive in Vietnam. Springtime cursed us with the assassinations of Martin Luther King and Robert Kennedy. Summer brought no relief as the Vietnam peace talks dragged on and anti-war protests intensified.

No doubt about it, 1968 was a year we would just as soon forget.

That is, except for Christmas Eve. A beacon of hope came to us that night, the thrill of accomplishment. For the first time in history men were orbiting the moon. And they were Americans!

We could hardly believe our eyes as television relayed the dramatic lunar vista beneath *Apollo 8*. Astronauts Frank Borman, James Lovell, and William Anders sent their Christmas greetings from a quarter million miles away. Then they read to us the first chapter of an old Book. Comforting words, somehow familiar and yet nearly forgotten: "In the beginning God created the heaven and the earth."

The *New York Times,* commenting on that Scripture reading from lunar orbit, observed, "Somehow it was exactly right."

Yes, what could have been more appropriate for our astronauts than to recognize that the blue sphere they looked back upon exists not by accident, but because God put it here?

Some months after the mission of *Apollo 8* I learned of a rather unusual incident that had taken place that Christmas Eve. Naturally, many reporters were present at the Space Center in Houston, some of them from foreign nations. Among them were two from a country without a Christian background. These men had been deeply impressed as the astronauts read from Genesis.

The stark splendor of those grand words touched their minds and hearts.

Not realizing they had been listening to Scripture, they approached someone from NASA and asked if a script from which the astronauts read might be available.

The American official replied with a meaningful smile, "Why, yes, when you get back to your hotel room, just open the drawer of your desk or your nightstand. You will find a book bound in black. And the script from which the astronauts read is on the very first page."

"In the beginning God created." Strange as it may seem, many Christians in America are not as moved by these immortal words as those atheist journalists were. Even many churchgoing scientists and educators, searching for the origins of life, find themselves unable to accept any answer that points to a Creator. They would gladly spend millions of dollars probing outer space to find our roots. They would welcome some ancient legend or embrace some dusty artifact.

But not the Bible account of creation!

They seem to enjoy bobbing like corks on the sea of uncertainty.

If they knew something for sure, they couldn't speculate anymore. All this to escape a Creator!

All this to escape moral responsibility?

I'm convinced that doubting God's Word is not just a problem of logic. It's more a problem of attitude. Human nature wants to "do its own thing," although we might not want to admit it. So we hide our doubts amid intellectual verbiage.

It was Aldous Huxley who said, "The philosopher who finds no meaning in the world is not concerned exclusively with a problem in pure metaphysics, he is also concerned to prove that there is no valid reason why he personally should not do as he wants to do."—*Ends and Means,* p. 315.

You see, if there is a Creator, then we stand accountable before Him who gave us life. But if we are only sophisticated animals, arriving here by chance, then we have no responsibility. We can do as we please. Or at least whatever we can get away with.

No doubt about it, a God powerful enough to create is unpopular in scientific circles. But lately we hear word of unrest among scientists. Not a few have come to realize that life is too complex to have sprung unannounced from a puddle of chemicals sparked by random lightning bolts. Here and there we find movement toward the Genesis account, what one writer calls "a sheepish resort" to the idea of a Creator.

Some scientists have stepped out boldly to declare their faith in the Bible account of creation. One of them, Robert Gentry, has caused quite a stir among his peers by his discovery of what one evolutionist calls "a tiny mystery."

We will discuss Gentry's fascinating discovery in a moment, but first let me tell you his story.

Bob Gentry had grown up in a Christian home believing the biblical account of life's origins. But while taking a freshman biology course at the University of Florida he began doubting the Scriptures. By the time he finished his studies there he had become a theistic evolutionist—one who disbelieves the Genesis creation account but still believes God exists.

One day an agnostic friend recommended a television program called "It Is Written." Gentry had no idea religion was involved until he tuned in to our telecast the next Sunday evening. But he then became one of our regular viewers.

When I visited Orlando in the spring of 1959 to conduct some lectures, the Gentrys invited me to their home. We discussed creation and evolution. I expressed my conviction that those who discard the account of Genesis also discredit the rest of the Bible. For instance, the Ten Commandments teach beyond question that God created the world in six literal days. We looked at the fourth commandment together:

"Remember the Sabbath day, to keep it holy. Six days you shall labor and do all your work, but the seventh day is the Sabbath of the Lord your God. In it you shall do no work: . . . For in six days the Lord made . . . the heavens and the earth. . . . Therefore the Lord blessed the sabbath day and hallowed it." Exodus 20:8-11.

This Sabbath commandment directly challenged Bob Gentry's confidence in evolution. He had been trying to maintain faith in the Bible by equating the six days of creation with six long geological eras. But now he realized that if such were the case, the commandment would be saying something like this:

"Six billion years you shall labor, and do all your work; but the seventh billion years is a sabbath of the Lord your God; in it you shall not do any work, . . . for in six billion years the Lord made heaven and earth . . . and rested the seventh billion years; therefore the Lord blessed the seventh billion years and hallowed it."

That gets a little ridiculous, wouldn't you say? Well, Bob Gentry thought so too.

So now he had a puzzle to solve. The Sabbath commandment proved that Genesis 1 required six twenty-four-hour days in the Creation week. But science seemed to indicate otherwise—radiometric dating appeared to prove the earth to be billions of years old.

This conflict between Scripture and science caused quite a dilemma for Gentry. At first he thought he must either reject the Bible as unreliable or surrender his belief in science. Instead, he decided to search out the scientific evidence to see for himself if it could be reconciled with the Creation account in God's Word.

Gentry began to realize that the case for evolution rested on shaky ground. Everything depended upon a questionable assumption known as the "uniformitarian principle." This theory supposes that the universe evolved through the ages by means of physical laws that have never changed.

If evidence could be found disproving this uniformitarian supposition, the evolutionary theory would fall apart. Geologists would have no basis for assuming that radioactive decay has been constant throughout history, no basis for believing the earth has existed for billions of years.

With these thoughts churning in his mind, Bob Gentry moved his family to the Atlanta area. There he taught physics while pursuing graduate studies at the Georgia Institute of Technology.

Gentry's quest for truth led him to investigate radioactive halos. (These are imprints of radioactivity in rocks which reveal the radiation present long ago when the earth came into existence.) But the department chairman wasn't enthusiastic about this new area of study. For a year he tried to discourage Gentry.

Finally he said, "Well, look, Bob. The time has come for me to tell you frankly, if you want to do this research, fine. But you can't do it at Georgia Tech. I don't think you're going to find anything. But what if you did? If you published evidence that disrupted the evolutionary time scale, what would happen to Georgia Tech? You would be an embarrassment to everyone."

And so Bob Gentry took his conscience away from Georgia Tech, forfeiting his doctoral dreams under those circumstances. Now, in the summer of 1964, he found himself nearly destitute, without a regular income. The family exhausted their savings as well as funds borrowed from relatives in launching new research into those promising radioactive halos. All for the sake of reconciling science with the Bible.

For the next few months things remained rather bleak for the Gentry family. Nothing much turned up in Bob's research. Then he began noticing under the microscope that certain rocks had unusual ring patterns. These mysterious "radiohalos" showed evidence of radioactivity with a fleeting existence. Lasting just a very brief time and then disappearing.

Bob explains it this way: "Suppose I have a glass of water and I put an Alka Seltzer tablet in it. The bubbles flow out and then disappear within just a few seconds. Either I freeze that water instantly and catch the bubbles in transit, or else they're gone forever.

"That's exactly what I was looking at under the microscope. Radioactivity in rapid transition, like those bubbles, had been quickly trapped in earth's foundation rocks. If those rocks had taken hundreds of thousands of years to cool and solidify, as evolutionists believed, these radiohalos could never have been formed. Something with such a fleeting existence must have been trapped in a matter of minutes. How had that happened?"

Finally one spring afternoon in 1965 Bob Gentry received his answer. Here's how he tells what happened:

"I was home alone with my three children. The house was silent—it was our "quiet hour," and my boisterous little ones were asleep. I moved my borrowed microscope from the back room to the front of the house to re-examine those fascinating halos.

"Suddenly, as I stared into the microscope, two verses from Scripture flashed into my mind: 'By the word of the Lord the heavens were made, and all the host of them by the breath of His mouth.' 'For He spoke, and it was done; He commanded, and it stood fast.' Psalm 33:6, 9.

"As I sat there stunned, a solution suggested itself. These radiohalos in earth's foundation rocks revealed radiation that had been active long ago but since had ceased. So what most geologists thought would have taken ages could have happened quite quickly. Could this be scientific evidence of an instantaneous creation event? Could these radiohalos, in a sense, be God's fingerprints?"

Evidently Bob Gentry was onto something here. Something really big!

Gradually he realized the tremendous implications of his discovery. He determined to test his findings by subjecting them to inspection by his peers in the world's most reputable scientific journals. Before anything could be published, it would have to survive cautious and critical analysis. And once in print, the article would be further scrutinized by evolutionists everywhere. Any errors in his methodology would be quickly exposed.

Gentry managed to publish more than twenty reports in noted scientific journals. The basic criticism he met was, "This can't be true because evolution is true." But his conclusions remained intact.

Eventually Bob Gentry came to be recognized as the world's foremost authority in his particular subspecialty. The U.S. Atomic Energy Commission invited him to do research at the Oak Ridge National Laboratory.

October 27, 1981, Gentry was at work in his office at Oak Ridge when the phone rang. The attorney general's office from the state of Arkansas was calling—they needed Gentry to testify at the forthcoming Arkansas creation trial as one of the expert science witnesses for the state. The teaching of creation in public schools had been opposed by the American Civil Liberties Union as being unscientific. Gentry was asked to help meet the challenge by presenting his scientific evidence for creation.

At the trial, Gentry's research was scrutinized again by some of the world's most distinguished evolutionists. Then it came time for the ACLU's geologist to be cross-examined. Asked specifically about the fleeting existence of radioactive halos, he conceded that evolution had no satisfactory explanation for them. The courtroom listened in awe as he could only say, "Gentry has found a tiny mystery which scientists some day will solve."

Yes, the testimony of earth's granite rock halos is creation's tiny mystery. But scientists will never solve it. They will never solve it because the Creator of the universe has placed in those halos His eternal fingerprints. Evidence that cannot be contradicted.

Many honest minds these days are becoming convinced about creation because of Bob Gentry. But whether or not we accept his compelling conclusions, one fact remains self-evident: It does matter what we believe about our beginnings. For what we believe about how we got here determines what we believe about God. If He has misled us in the Bible about creation, how can He be a God worth worshiping?

And what we believe about our beginnings determines what we believe about the future. For if we discard the book of Genesis as myth and legend, why should we take the prophecies of Revelation seriously?

What we believe about our origin affects what we believe about ourselves; it affects our sense of self-worth. For if we just evolved from some lowly cell in the sea, we would not have the dignity of being formed in the image of God. And if the human race did not fall from that high position, if Adam didn't sin, then why did we need a Saviour for the human race? The mission of Jesus becomes pointless and the cross only a meaningless drama!

We could go on and on. I think you can see that what we

believe about our beginnings could well determine our eternal destiny. Is it any wonder that the devil, fighting against our souls, aims his sharpest arrows at the first seven chapters of Genesis?

Why is this generation, obsessed with piecing together our beginnings; why is it looking everywhere but in God's Word? There can be only one answer. It wants to find Adam. But it doesn't want to find him in Genesis!

Yet all the while the simple statement of Scripture stands firm, quietly inviting our faith: "In the beginning God created."

Could it be that the evidence collected by Bob Gentry and many others was left by the Creator to help establish faith in the Genesis account? After all, the Bible itself says; "Now faith is the substance of things hoped for, the evidence of things not seen." Hebrews 11:1.

Though the Genesis account will never be proven beyond question, God has given all the evidence we need for strong confidence in His creation.

Doubt is in the air. But so are the birds, who fly above us better equipped for navigation than the latest air force fighter jets, able to traverse unmapped oceans with their built-in instruments.

Controversy swirls around us. But so do the bats, who effortlessly operate their ultrasonic radar, reminding us that neither technology nor wisdom are exclusive with the human mind.

Skepticism encircles the earth. But so do the stars, speeding along in their unerring orbits, keeping their appointments with a precision that boggles the mind.

Book after book insists authoritatively that this earth evolved over millions of years. Evolutionists talk confidently about the magic of the ages, of happy accidents that exploded us ever upward—with never a need for intelligent direction, never a need for God. But all the while birds and bats and the stars eloquently challenge their entrenched beliefs.

Long ago David proclaimed, "The heavens declare the glory of God; and the firmament shows His handiwork. Day unto day utters speech, and night unto night reveals knowledge. There is no speech nor language where their voice is not heard." Psalm 19:1-3.

Nobody can escape the grand harmony as all nature joins in the unmistakable chorus, "There is a Creator!" But the One who made this world also let His creatures nail Him to a rough, splintery cross outside Jerusalem —so that lost sinners might find eternal life in Him. And even the evidence of the birds and the bats, of suns and racing constellations, convincing as it is, pales before the mighty argument of the cross!

You may have heard the story of the unbeliever who rescued an orphan boy from a burning building. Having lost his own wife and child, he wanted to adopt the lad.

Christian neighbors were skeptical about the wisdom of placing the boy in an infidel home. But the applicant won his case when he held up his hand, badly burned in the rescue of the lad, and said, "I have only one argument. It is this."

He proved to be a good father, and little Jimmy never tired of hearing how Daddy had saved him from the fire. And he liked best to hear about the scarred hand.

One day with his new father he visited a display of art masterpieces. One painting interested him especially—the one of Jesus reproving Thomas for his unbelief and holding out His scarred hand.

"Tell me the story of that picture, Daddy," the little fellow pleaded.

"No, not that one."

"Why not?"

"Because I don't believe it."

"But you tell me the story of Jack the giant-killer, and you don't believe that."

So he told him the story. And Jimmy said, "It's like you and me, Daddy." And then he went on, "It wasn't nice of Thomas not to believe after the good Man had died for him. What if they had told me how you saved me from the fire and I had said I didn't believe you did it?"

The father could not escape the sound reasoning of a little child. He had used his own scarred hand to win a small boy's heart.

Could he continue to resist the scarred hand of the Man who had died for him—and say He didn't do it?

The mightiest argument of all is the cross of Calvary. The scarred hands of Jesus. Hands that were wounded in His encounter with the forces of evil—so that you and I could live!

What can we do but fall at His feet and say with Thomas, "My Lord and my God!"

When God Made Rest

How long has it been since you've taken a walk in the woods? Or spent an hour beside a secluded waterfall—just watching, relaxing, letting it tumble away your cares? How long has it been since you've backpacked deep into the wilderness? Have you forgotten what it's like?

Just thinking about it refreshes you. And looking through your favorite book of nature photos will set you planning for the first free weekend that comes your way.

You'll turn off the ignition and step into silence. Silence broken only by the sound of some little wild creature of the woods. Or a bird song that you haven't heard since childhood. You walk softly, slowly, listening after every step. You want to see the next bird that you hear.

But a bluejay noisily broadcasts your presence. Now all the forest knows you are coming. Might as well let the twigs snap.

The hours slip happily by as you gather up memories to keep forever. There's plenty of time in the wilderness. Time to sit on a moss-covered log and get acquainted with nature again—with life again. Time to climb the nearest mountain, to look down at where you've been, and up to heights you've never seen before.

Time to mount your high-powered binoculars on a tripod

and watch wildlife in action—creatures who wouldn't perform if they knew you were in the audience. Time to watch a coyote leap high in the air and come down mouth first, mouth wide open, emerging with a gopher and a mouthful of dirt.

Time to watch a snowshoe hare, his nose twitching. Moose dunking their heads in a beaver pond. A brown mink hiding fish for its dinner beneath a rock in a tiny pool. A sandhill crane catching mice and insects. Time to watch a swift, graceful fox and see the mischief in his eyes as he turns your way. A little black bear that seems to be daring you to come one step closer. You feel as if you're cheating, seeing it all so close!

There's time to follow any trail you choose—or no trail at all. You have no appointments in the wild. You don't have to go anywhere. Says Les Blacklock, whose colorful phrases I have been borrowing, "If you want to get somewhere, don't follow a wildlife trail. Moose trails run into bear trails, bear trails into deer trails, deer trails into fox trails, fox trails into rabbit trails, rabbit trails into squirrel trails, and they go up a tree and into a hole."

Finally, as the sun drops low in the west, you are perched on a boulder beside a waterfall, enjoying your supper. Why couldn't you always live like this? But tomorrow it's back to the grind. Yet all this beauty, all this discovery, is stored in your mind. Nothing can take it away. You go back to work refreshed.

Just think about it. If we find nature so enjoyable in this world of sin and death, imagine what the great outdoors was like for Adam and Eve in their unpolluted paradise.

Come with me back to the Garden of Eden. It's late Friday afternoon of creation week. God had just crowned His wonderful work by forming children in His own image. Tenderly He shares with them His own breath of life. And now He introduces Himself.

Can you imagine the feeling when Adam and Eve meet their Creator?

Then hand in hand together they explore their paradise home. Beauty beyond belief delights and dazzles their senses. Lush green meadows, clear-running streams, and breathtaking scenery surpassing description.

And no crime. No slums or prisons or hospitals. No rat race to attend to. Nothing but calm and peace.

As Adam and Eve gaze in awe at the splendors of Eden, the Lord turns it over to their care. But before they take charge of their beautiful garden, the Creator sets up a weekly appointment with them.

And so we read: "Then God blessed the seventh day and sanctified it, because in it He rested from all His work which God had created and made." Genesis 2:3.

Did God "sanctify," or set apart, the seventh day because He was tired? Or because He considers our relationship with Him important enough to deserve that special day every week? We can get so involved with the daily routine, so trapped in trivia, that we forget what's most important—our relationship with our Lord. That's why He gave us the Sabbath.

God also knew we need a weekly reservation to be with our loved ones, uninterrupted by daily duties. Often family members brush past each other throughout the busy week, out of time and out of touch, nearly strangers in the same home. So each week the Sabbath offers time off together from the cares of life to refresh family relationships.

We can see why Jesus said, "The Sabbath . . . was made for man's sake." Mark 2:27, Phillips. If Adam and Eve needed Sabbath rest in paradise, how much more we need it now!

Let's take a closer look at the special day God gave us. It involves more than relief from the rat race and an opportunity for spiritual and family fellowship. The timing of the Sabbath carries deep spiritual significance. Let me explain.

God, you recall, finished creation in six days and rested the seventh. Then He invited His children to share the celebration of His work, even though they had done nothing to earn the right to rest.

They accepted God's accomplishment on their behalf, resting with Him as if they had performed the work themselves.

This Sabbath rest in God's finished work symbolizes what Christianity stands for. Other world religions focus upon human "realization"—what we can do to help ourselves. But Christians celebrate God's accomplishments on our behalf. That's why the Sabbath points us away from ourselves, away from our works, so we can value what God has done.

But human nature tends to doubt God and question what He gives us. Satan, working through the serpent, deceived Adam and Eve with the delusion that God was holding something back from them. Something was lacking in what He provided.

You know the sad story. Adam and Eve succumbed at the tree and abandoned God's plan for their happiness. Picture the scene as Adam and Eve linger under the tree, savoring the flavor of forbidden fruit. Suddenly, chills race up their spines. Icy pangs of guilt.

Shivering in their shame, they hunt refuge in the depths of the forest. There they hastily stitch together garments of fig leaves, trying to cover over the nakedness of their sin.

Then, as they crouch amid their lush green prison, terror overwhelms them. They remember God's warning. He had told them that on the day they strayed from Him they must die—and here He comes to kill them!

But no, God doesn't strike them dead. Instead He tenderly covers their shame with the skin of an animal.

What's happening here? Why does He let them live? —Or did they really die that day after all?

Think it through. What must you do in order to have a garment of skin? You need to kill. An innocent animal, maybe a lamb, died the death of that guilty couple at the gates of the Garden of Eden.

Because a substitute perished in their place, they could live. A happy life, free from the burden of condemnation.

You know who that sacrificial lamb symbolized—our Lord Jesus Christ, the great Lamb of God. Through His death for us on the cross He earned our salvation. And this plan of redemption was revealed way back at the gates of the Garden of Eden. Every bleeding lamb on Old Testament altars reminded repenting sinners to trust in the blood of their Saviour to come.

Let's go reverently now to Golgotha outside old Jerusalem, known as the place of the skull. It's another Friday afternoon—we call it "Good Friday." Amid the scorn of His enemies and the mournful unbelief of His friends, Jesus hangs in open shame on the cross. The Lord of glory is offering His life as the substitute for doomed humanity. He's accomplishing the work of our salvation.

Now it's late in the afternoon. Life is fading fast. With His dying breath Jesus cries, "It is finished!"

Is this a wail of despair? No, not at all! It's the triumphant announcement of a completed task. Mission accomplished! Mankind redeemed!

As the sun begins to set, the friends of Jesus lay Him lovingly to rest inside a tomb. There He remains over the Sabbath hours to memorialize His work of salvation. After His quiet Sabbath repose, Jesus resurrects and ascends to the throne of God.

We can see why Jesus proclaimed Himself "Lord of the Sabbath." Because the Sabbath commemorates His two greatest acts on our behalf—creating us and saving us. These are the reasons we worship Him. And we express our faith in Christ as our Maker and Redeemer by sharing His Sabbath rest. Every Friday evening as the sun goes down, millions of Christians around the world stop working. They set aside their unfinished business to celebrate the finished work of Jesus.

What therapy for legalism we find in the Sabbath! The enemy of souls well knows that many who try to please God wind up trusting in their own works for salvation. They rummage around in their lives for evidence that they deserve to go to heaven. Then, overwhelmed by their failure to measure up to Christ's character, they cry out in despair, "Woe is me, for I am undone!" Many give up hope and return to the old life of sin.

The Sabbath is designed by God to prevent spiritual discouragement. Week by week the seventh day comforts our conscience, assuring us that despite our unfinished characters we stand complete in Christ. His accomplishment at Calvary counts as our atonement. We enter His rest.

But many sincere followers of Jesus don't understand the Sabbath. They consider God's day of rest an ancient Jewish relic with no meaning for modern Christians. Some even regard Sabbathkeeping as an attempt to gain salvation by works. Yet nothing could be further from the truth. You see, the word *Sabbath* comes from a Hebrew word meaning "to cease, desist, rest"—the very opposite of works.

Of course, works of love are essential in Christian living; it's just that we don't depend upon them for salvation. In appreciation for salvation by grace, genuine faith leads us to be faithful and obedient. You may be aware that many Christians are having second thoughts about neglecting God's law. After decades of being taught that the Ten Commandments have been done away with, we are reaping a society cursed with crime, devoid of law and order. And so we've finally realized that moral absolutes are essential.

We need God's law. But we are not saved through that law. We're saved by trusting in Jesus—and that's the message of the Sabbath.

Have you ever noticed that the Sabbath commandment

differs from the other nine? All the other commandments tell us what we must do for God and neighbor. But the Sabbath points us away from human works—to rest in *God's* work for us. And that's the gospel! Without Sabbath rest, our obedience to God would indeed be legalism.

No doubt about it, the Sabbath is the greatest teaching tool of the gospel. It's the brightest of billboards proclaiming Calvary's freedom. Week by week the seventh day comes around to remind us we can't save ourselves—we must trust Jesus. And in this world where atheism abounds, the Sabbath testifies that we didn't evolve by chance. God made us as His children.

One afternoon a friend of mine was sharing his testimony at California State University in Northridge, near Los Angeles. Ted, a sophomore art student, wanted to know why the Bible insists he become a Christian.

Hindus and Buddhists have high moral standards," he argued. "Moslems and Jews worship a personal God. Certainly Jesus was a wonderful man, but couldn't we just appreciate Him as a person and remain outside of Christanity?"

"Not really," my friend responded. "Many world religions value Christ as a teacher and a worthy example. But only Christianity points to Him as the divine Saviour and Creator."

These twin facts of life—creation and salvation, form the foundation of genuine religion. And God has memorialized both of them by the seventh-day Sabbath, the day of our Lord Jesus Christ.

Are you beginning to see what that special day at the end of the week is all about? A happy reminder that we are not the children of chance, but children of the heavenly King! And a promise that through Christ's saving sacrifice the human family will enjoy paradise restored.

Did you know that through all eternity the Sabbath will bring us together for worship?

" 'For as the new heavens and the new earth which I will

make shall remain before Me,' says the Lord, 'so shall your descendants and your name remain. And it shall come to pass that from one New Moon to another, and from one Sabbath to another, all flesh shall come to worship before Me,' saith the Lord." Isaiah 66:22, 23.

Wonderful news, wouldn't you say? Forever we will have our name—our personal identity—and our descendents, our children. We will enjoy heaven with our families! And all of us together will worship our Lord on His Sabbath day.

Just picture that first glorious Sabbath in heaven with Jesus. What will it be like to have Him lead the morning worship service? To hear the angel choir. Then to take an afternoon stroll with our Saviour along the river of life.

I can hardly wait for heaven, can you?

But tell me. If we will worship together on God's holy Sabbath throughout the ceaseless ages of eternity, why not begin right now?

A Day
to Remember

May I take you back nearly two thousand years to the humble village of Nazareth in Palestine? It is midweek as we make our way down the narrow cobblestone street, past the little shops with their open fronts. We see workmen plying their trades while we pass one shop after another. A leisurely Middle Eastern atmosphere pervades the town.

As we walk along, we notice a shop that is different. The front has been neatly whitewashed and the street recently swept. We enter and find a kindly, stalwart man plying the carpenter's trade, and by his side a young assistant—we would guess about eighteen years of age.

The young man is planing a piece of wood, making it true, making it straight. He rests a moment and wipes his brow. As He turns, we see He has the bearing of a prince, of a king. For He is none other than the Prince of heaven, King Jesus, come here to cast His lot with the poor, to live and work among humanity and die in our place.

We hurry on. But we come back again, for we are fascinated by the little shop. We come back on Thursday. We come back on Friday. We come back on Saturday.

But on Saturday the shop is closed. The tools have been carefully put away. The shavings have been gathered up from the floor. All is quiet. We notice that the people are all walking toward a conspicuous building in the center of the village. Following them, we find our seats in the rear of a well-filled meetinghouse.

We wait a moment. Then to our surprise we see the carpenter's Son make His way into the pulpit, open the scroll, and begin to read. Are we imagining all this? No. The Gospel of Luke tells us something about the worship habits of Jesus:

"So He came to Nazareth, where He had been brought up. And as His custom was, He went into the synagogue on the Sabbath day, and stood up to read." Luke 4:16.

What are we watching here? Someone dutifully conforming to the customs of His day—customs acceptable for His generation but not for ours? Or are we watching the One who has set the example for all Christians to follow?

Is this a young Jewish carpenter thoughtlessly complying with the traditions of His time? Or rather the Creator, resting on the day He Himself set apart for the human family?

What is the truth about Jesus and the Sabbath? Why do we have such confusion about the Lord's Day? Does it really matter which day we observe as the Sabbath? Or is any day acceptable to God—Friday, Saturday, or Sunday?

Let me share a personal experience that taught me a valuable lesson. A few years ago as a college student (quite a few years, I must say) I was traveling the highways from Detroit to New York City.

Having passed Toledo and Cleveland, and being not far away from Pittsburgh, I *knew* where I was going. Straight through to Philadelphia and on to New York. You couldn't possibly have convinced me I wasn't bound for New York City.

Well, do you know what happened? A Greyhound bus, loaded with people and plainly marked "New York City," passed me—going in the opposite direction!

My mind snapped to attention. "Either that bus driver is

confused, or I'm mistaken." Suddenly I wasn't so sure about my sense of direction. And in this case, my confusion was a good thing, as I discovered after driving off the highway into a service station.

I put my question in a way that would bring the answer I wanted, just as children do so often. Pointing ahead, I asked the station attendant, "Isn't that the way to New York City?"

"Yes," he agreed, "but it's 25,000 miles that way. And there's a lot of water in between. I'd suggest you try the opposite direction if you really want to get to New York."

Well, what a surprise! Evidently I had driven out of a restaurant or a service station the wrong way, without realizing I had turned back the way I came.

Friend, tell me. Could it be possible that somebody has turned the Sabbath sign around—and some of us didn't know it? I ask again, does it make a difference which day a person keeps as the Sabbath? Is just any day acceptable to God?

Why don't we open our Bibles to find out. Three texts together will provide the answer for us. In the New Testament book of Revelation we read:

"I was in the Spirit on the Lord's Day, and I heard behind me a loud voice, as of a trumpet." Revelation 1:10.

Now this verse doesn't tell us a great deal. It's simply a statement of fact. John the disciple was under the Spirit's influence on the Lord's day.

But one thing we do learn here, something stated quite clearly, is that the Lord does have a day. Now, it doesn't tell us here which one of the seven is the Lord's day. Just that God has one day set apart from the rest. We can no longer imagine that it doesn't matter which day we keep, as long as we just keep one day in seven. So the Bible speaks of a particular day called the Lord's day.

Which day could this be? We find out in our next text:

"The Son of Man is Lord even of the Sabbath." Matthew 12:8.

This is getting interesting. We've already noticed that the Lord has a day which He calls His own. And here this verse says that Jesus is "Lord . . . of the Sabbath." So the Sabbath is the Lord's day, according to Christ's own words.

But which day of the seven is the Bible Sabbath?

Let's go to our third text. You will recognize this immediately as one of the Ten Commandments:

"Remember the Sabbath day, to keep it holy. Six days you shall labor and do all your work, but the seventh day is the Sabbath of the Lord your God." Exodus 20:8-10.

Here we have it all put together in a single sentence: The Lord has a day; that day is the Sabbath; and the seventh day is the Sabbath. God considers the Sabbath so important that He made it one of His Ten Commandments.

Now let me ask you once more: When Jesus went into the meetinghouse on that Sabbath, was He just a carpenter mechanically following the traditions of His time? Or was He our Creator resting on the day that He Himself had made?

Surprising as it may seem, did you know that Jesus Himself made the Sabbath? The Bible identifies Him as our Creator. We read in John 1:10:

"He was in the world, and the world was made through Him, and the world did not know Him."

So the world was made through Him, by Him. But who is this speaking of? Verse 1 tells us, "In the beginning was the Word, and the Word was with God, and the Word was God." Then verse 14 says, "The Word became flesh and dwelt among us, and we beheld His glory, the glory as of the only begotten of the Father, full of grace and truth."

The Word of God who spoke the world into existence can be none other than Jesus Christ. Long before His birth in Bethlehem, He created this world and set apart the seventh day. The Christ of Calvary is the Creator of Genesis—and the

Lord of the Sabbath. *To reject one is to reject the other.*

You can see, then, that the Sabbath involves more than a dispute over days. It isn't an irrelevant hangover from a forgotten past.

This is the New Testament Lord's day, the day of our Lord Jesus Christ.

Throughout His life on earth, Christ faithfully kept the Sabbath.

Does all this surprise you? Have you been conditioned to think that Jesus attached little importance to the Sabbath?

Quite a controversy rages throughout the gospels over Jesus and the Sabbath. Prevailing traditions had shackled the Sabbath with rigid rules and burdensome requirements that Jesus had no use for.

Continually He found Himself at odds with the religious establishment over His behavior on the Sabbath. One typical confrontation we find recorded in Mark 3:1-6:

"He entered the synagogue again, and a man was there who had a withered hand. And they [the priests] watched Him closely, whether He would heal him on the Sabbath, so that they might accuse Him."

Jesus might have avoided this controversy over the Sabbath. But He couldn't pass by this opportunity to display the creative power that had made the world—He wanted to draw His audience toward faith in His divinity for the sake of their salvation.

Picture the scene as Jesus took command of the situation:

"He said to the man who had the withered hand, 'Step forward.' And He said to them [the priests], 'Is it lawful on the Sabbath to do good or to do evil, to save life or to kill?'

"But they kept silent."

"So when He had looked around at them with anger, being grieved by the hardness of their hearts, He said to the man, 'Stretch out your hand.'

"And he stretched it out, and his hand was restored as

whole as the other. Then the Pharisees went out and immediately plotted with the Herodians against Him, how they
might destroy Him."

Again and again Jesus risked His life to display the creative power of which the Sabbath is a memorial. So essential
is a proper understanding of Sabbath rest that Jesus let it
become a life-or-death matter in His dealings with the religious establishment. He entered into a showdown that eventually climaxed at the cross. That's how important the Sabbath was to Jesus.

Sometimes we can best determine the strength of a
leader's convictions by watching his followers. Shall we,
then, move down to the close of Christ's ministry, to that
tragic Friday afternoon of the crucifixion? Let's observe His
associates as they come up to the sunset hour. Their Lord has
been laid in the tomb, and the Sabbath is approaching.

Christ's followers may have been careful about the Sabbath in the past, but what will they do now? Their hopes had
been bitterly blasted that day. No words can describe the
depths of their despondency, and I need not tell you that de-
spondent people are often careless people. And if ever they
were tempted to ignore the sacred hours, it was now.

Yes, if anything in the example of Jesus encouraged care-
lessness about the Sabbath, we would surely detect it now in
the attitude of His closest friends. But let's look at what happened:

"This man [Joseph, a Jewish leader who was becoming a
disciple] went to Pilate and asked for the body of Jesus. Then
he took it down, wrapped it in linen, and laid it in a tomb
that was hewn out of the rock, where no one had ever lain
before.

"That day was the Preparation, and the Sabbath drew
near. And the women who had come with Him from Galilee
followed after, and they observed the tomb and how His body
was laid. Then they returned and prepared spices and fra-

grant oils. And they rested on the Sabbath according to the commandment.

"Now on the first day of the week, very early in the morning, they, and certain other women with them, came to the tomb bringing the spices which they had prepared." Luke 23:52—24:1.

From this passage we can only conclude that the reverence of Christ's followers for the Sabbath hours reflected the reverence of their Lord. If Jesus had any doubts about the continuing importance of the Sabbath, He had utterly failed to communicate it to those who knew Him best. Nothing He did, nothing He taught, revealed anything but total respect for the day over which He proclaimed Himself the Lord.

Well, at this point you may be wondering how we can know which day was the seventh day, the day Jesus and His followers kept.

I once asked that question of an audience. And I must have stopped to catch my breath or something. I had just said, "How can we know that the Saturday of today is the seventh day of Christ's time?"

Just as I paused, someone exclaimed so that all could hear, "That's what I want to know!"

You might be surprised that the Bible verses we just read identify the Sabbath. For notice that three consecutive days are mentioned: the preparation day, the Sabbath of the commandment, and the first day of the week. Two are given sacred titles. "The preparation day," "the Sabbath of the commandment," and one is given an ordinary number, "the first day of the week." Or to put it another way—the day of the crucifixion, the day Jesus rested in the tomb, and, finally, the day on which He was resurrected.

The Bible tells us Jesus died and then rose the third day.

Nothing has been better established among Christian scholars than that Jesus was crucified on the day we now call Good Friday and was resurrected on the day we look back upon as Easter Sunday. The "Sabbath of the commandment" is the day between Friday and Sunday. And of course that is our Saturday. Could anything be more simple?

But what about the centuries since that time? Can we really know whether the seventh-day Sabbath of Christ's time is still the same seventh day of the week we know today?

A fascinating fact confirming today's Saturday as the Bible Sabbath is this: In more than 100 languages the word for the seventh day of the week is the national word for Sabbath. In Spanish, for example, *Sabado* is the seventh day of the week. You don't have to be Hispanic to recognize that the word means "Sabbath." In Russian, the word for the seventh day is also the translation of Sabbath.

That's even true with Hindustani, a language of India.

All these languages the world over confirm that calendar changes have not affected our weekly cycle. The Bible Sabbath is still the seventh day today, our Saturday—the special day of our Lord Jesus Christ.

This brings us to the big question. Since the Bible so plainly teaches that the seventh day, our Saturday, is the Sabbath of the Lord, how is it that most Christians keep the first day of the week?

Who changed the Sabbath to Sunday?

We shall find out in our next several chapters as centuries tell their story since the day He died. But now shall we pause a moment to consider what we've seen so far? Perhaps this is the first time you have investigated the truth about the seventh-day Sabbath. Your mind may be full of questions.

But one thing is clear: when we truly love Jesus, we will accept every ray of light He shines upon us. Wouldn't you say? And we will take His hand as He leads us in His Word, calling us, "Follow Me!"

Following Jesus—isn't that the test of our Christianity?

Since the Day He Died

Would you turn your thoughts back a few years to the day our nation suddenly stood still? Black Friday, November 22, 1963.

First word of the tragedy in Dallas came when bulletins interrupted the routine dilemmas of the soap operas. In newsrooms across the country, editors grabbed up wire releases from teletype machines, holding their breath and fearing the worst. Finally came the terrible confirmation. Our beloved president was dead!

Newscasters couldn't control their emotions. People sobbed in the streets as the awful word spread. Shoppers went home. The stock market closed.

We were stunned, bewildered, brokenhearted. But somehow we rallied, and life went on. Uncounted memorials sprang up across the land. Jacqueline Kennedy lit the eternal flame. Highways, stadiums, and airports were named after our fallen leader. Cape Canaveral became Cape Kennedy. Lyndon Johnson felt that the most fitting memorial would be to carry out the program interrupted by the Dallas bullet. And so he declared, "Let us continue!"

However inadequate the parallel, on another black Friday long ago our Lord Jesus Christ was assassinated. But His death was a glorious victory. Calvary sealed the everlasting covenant, guaranteeing salvation to sinners everywhere willing to come to Him. And three days later He burst forth from the tomb as the conquering King.

Are there memorials given by God to honor the life and death of Jesus? Millions of sincere Christians keep Sunday in honor of His resurrection. And why not memorialize the day of the empty tomb? It seems so natural, so right.

But should we not ask a question here? Has the keeping of Sunday been sanctioned by God? The Bible is our guide in these things. To satisfactorily answer this question, let's examine each scripture in the New Testament that says anything at all about the first day of the week. This should help set our minds at rest and dispel some of the confusion.

We don't want to do this in the spirit of trying to prove something. We just want to know what our Lord desires us to do—what our relationship with Him requires of us.

Surprising as it may seem, the New Testament mentions the first day of the week only eight times. Five of these texts mention that Christ arose on the first day of the week, a fact nobody questions.

But do we find in them any command, or even a suggestion, to keep holy that first day of the week?

Let's open its pages and see for ourselves. First we come to Matthew 28:1:

"After the Sabbath, as the first day of the week began to dawn, Mary Magdalene and the other Mary came to see the tomb."

A simple statement of fact. But notice that the first day of the week begins to dawn after the Sabbath. In this scripture, at least, there is certainly no divine direction asking us to keep the first day of the week as the Sabbath. Now the next reference, Mark 16:2:

"Very early in the morning, on the first day of the week, they came to the tomb when the sun had risen."

Again just a factual reference to the time of the resurrection.

The third scripture citing the first day of the week is right here in this same chapter, verse 9:

"Now when He rose early on the first day of the week, He appeared first to Mary Magdalene, out of whom He had cast seven demons."

Familiar words. Again no reference to a Sunday sacredness whatever, would you say?

The next two verses about the first day of the week, Luke 24:1 and John 20:1, only repeat what the others have said. Not much success yet in finding anything that authorizes keeping the first day of the week as the Lord's day. And remember that these scriptures call the Sabbath by its sacred title and the first day of the week by a simple number— "first day."

Our sixth mention of the first day of the week is in John 20:19:

"Then, the same day at evening, being the first day of the week, when the doors were shut where the disciples were assembled, for fear of the Jews, Jesus came and stood in the midst, and said to them, 'Peace be with you.' "

What do we have here, a resurrection rally? Suppose the disciples had gathered to celebrate the resurrection. Would that change the Sabbath to Sunday? Hardly. But notice that Christ's followers had gathered behind closed doors, not for a resurrection rally, but "for fear of the Jews." Jesus came to dispel their unbelief and convince them He was alive.

Just two more references left. Acts 20:7 says:

"Now on the first day of the week, when the disciples came together to break bread, Paul, ready to depart the next day, spoke to them and continued his message until midnight."

Here we find Paul preaching a farewell sermon on the first day of the week with the breaking of bread. Does this communion service indicate that the first day of the week had become holy? Keep in mind that Christ Himself instituted the Lord's Supper on a Thursday night. And that, of course, does not make Thursday the Sabbath.

Here's something else about Acts 20:7. This farewell meeting on the dark part of the first day of the week actually took place on what we now call Saturday night. Remember, the first day of the week begins at Sabbath sundown. A number of Bible versions even translate this meeting as being on Saturday night. Evidently Paul had been preaching on the Sabbath, according to his custom, and he "continued his message until midnight."

Now we come to the last New Testament reference to the first day of the week. It is in 1 Corinthians 16:2:

"On the first day of the week let each one of you lay something aside, storing up as he may prosper, that there be no collections when I come."

Is Paul here taking up a collection at church on the first day of the week? Notice those words "lay something aside, storing up." This passage doesn't even discuss a worship meeting at all. It's about storing up money on the first day of the week, before the week's allowance is gone, so the believers would have something saved up to give Paul when he came to visit.

You see, many Christians take care of life's necessities and entertainment, then finally—if anything happens to be left over—they remember the Lord's work. Paul says, "Don't do that—put God first in your finances. On the first day of the week, before you spend the week's money, set something aside for the poor, so that you'll have a good offering ready when I come."

So there we have it. Every scripture in the New Testament that mentions the first day of the week, Sunday. Did we find any Bible authority for Sunday sacredness? I think you will agree that Sunday keeping has not been authorized by God. It simply isn't scriptural.

Let's consider something else here. Something quite significant—the silence of the New Testament concerning any change in the day of rest by Christ or the apostles. That silence is deafening! Let me explain what I mean.

You know how much controversy Paul stirred up by teaching that circumcision was done away with. Can you imagine the uproar if the apostle had taught that the Sabbath was done away with?

Think about it.

Circumcision had for its authority only the ceremonial law, sometimes called the law of Moses—a law of sacrifices and ceremonies that ended when Jesus, the true Sacrifice, the Lamb of God, gave His life. Circumcision is not even mentioned in the Ten Commandments.

Imagine, if you can, the clamor that would have been raised if any change of the Sabbath, one of God's Ten Commandments, had been attempted or even suggested. We could expect to find many chapters, probably entire books, concerning the matter.

And remember that the New Testament was written from 19 to 63 years after the cross. Yet there is nothing but silence regarding worship on the first day of the week, even many years after the resurrection. At no time did anyone ever accuse Christ or the apostles of keeping any other day besides the Sabbath.

Nothing but silence about Sunday. Deafening silence.

Significant, don't you think?

At this point you may be told something like this: "Well, all right, the New Testament doesn't establish Sunday as the Lord's day. But as long as you take one day in seven, that's just fine with God."

But is it really? Does God give us permission to make truth suit ourselves? Is the Bible something like a cafeteria, where we pick and choose what we like and reject the rest?

Secular humanism teaches that moral matters, including religion, have no absolutes; everything is relative. Many

Christians condemn secular humanists for believing this way—yet do they not commit the same mistake themselves when it comes to the Sabbath?

Strange, wouldn't you say?

The truth is that we must worship God on His own terms—or reject Him entirely. And the same Jesus who created us and redeemed us gave us the Sabbath to memorialize those twin facts of life.

"But hasn't the Sabbath been replaced under the new covenant?" someone asks. Let's look into this. What about the old covenant and the new covenant? What's the difference between the two?

We find the first mention of a covenant in the Bible in Genesis, when the world became so wicked that God had to destroy it with a flood. "But Noah found grace in the eyes of the Lord." Genesis 6:8.

Based on that grace, the Lord spared Noah's life and established with him a treaty of spiritual partnership known as the "everlasting covenant." Genesis 9:16.

Later, God approached Abraham with this same everlasting covenant. See Genesis 17:7. One night He called Abraham outside his tent and urged him to look upward toward the desert sky. See the stars? God asked. "So shall your descendants be." Abraham "believed in the Lord, and He accounted it to him for righteousness." Genesis 15:5, 6.

Notice that Abraham's covenant was based on belief, not works.

Many think God saved people in Old Testament times through their works, and then in the New Testament He switched things around and introduced salvation by faith. That wouldn't be fair, would it? And it's also not true. The gospel of grace runs clear through the Old Testament like a refreshing mountain stream. Take the experience of Abraham and his son Isaac at Mount Moriah, that mountain of sacrifice. The aged father trembles at the thought of losing his only son. Then he remembers the gospel: "My son, God will provide for Himself the lamb for a burnt offering." Genesis 22:8.

God Himself provides the sacrifice for sin. That's our hope today. And their hope too, way back in Genesis and Exodus.

Unfortunately, Abraham's descendants forgot the gospel while suffering as slaves in Egypt. But in their distress they cried out to heaven. "God heard their groaning, and remembered His covenant with Abraham." Exodus 2:24. Through one of the most dramatic events of history—opening up the Red Sea—God delivered them from bondage.

After bringing His people safely across from danger, God led them in the wilderness to Mount Sinai. In that majestic setting He intended to renew with them the same everlasting covenant of grace already established with Noah and Abraham. He introduced the covenant by reminding His people of what He had just done to save them:

"You have seen what *I did* to the Egyptians, and how *I* . . . brought you to Myself. Now therefore, if you will indeed obey My voice and keep My covenant, then you shall be a special treasure to Me." Exodus 19:4, 5. Emphasis supplied.

God wanted the Israelites to accept *His* work for their salvation. But they didn't even wait to find out what kind of covenant He was talking about. Impulsively they declared, "All that the Lord has spoken *we* will do." Exodus 19:8.

This sounds good—they wanted to obey, didn't they? But there was a serious problem. The people were putting hope in their own performance rather than trusting in God's promises. The Lord had no interest in changing His covenant based on grace to a covenant based upon human works. So He carefully explained the high demands of His holy law, hoping the Israelites would realize what they were trying to get themselves into.

Before announcing His Ten Commandments, God tried one more time to impress them with what He had already done to save them: "I am the Lord your God, who brought you out of the land of Egypt, out of the house of bondage." Exodus 20:2.

But still they felt no need for trusting in God rather than in themselves. Still they insisted on righteousness by their works. "All that the Lord has said we will do," they repeated. Exodus 24:7.

This response ignored everything God had been emphasizing about His works for their salvation. No appreciation whatever for the everlasting covenant of grace.

Often our children have to learn the hard way. Broken toys and broken bones sometimes result, with many tears. The children of Israel also had to learn the hard way at Mount Sinai. God knew what would happen, but He let them exercise their free choice and have their covenant of works. Something quite different from the covenant of grace He had made with Abraham.

The results were tragic. A few days after making those wonderful promises, the Israelites found themselves dancing around in a wild orgy, worshiping the golden calf. Can you picture the scene! All their promises and resolutions proved to be no stronger than ropes of sand. Their useless covenant of works lay shattered in the desert sand.

Humbled and chastened, the Israelites were finally ready to hear the gospel. God explained the meaning of sacrificial lambs, just as He had done with Adam and Eve at the gates of the Garden of Eden.

Every bleeding lamb on the altar reminded them to trust for salvation in the blood of their Saviour to come.

And centuries later, when Jesus came to this earth, He fulfilled a new covenant. A different covenant based upon "better promises" than the old covenant established at Sinai. See Hebrews 8:6. Better promises because God made them, not frail humanity.

Here's something interesting: Christ's sacrifice was the

"blood of the everlasting covenant." Hebrews 13:20. Actually, the same covenant of grace established long before with Noah and Abraham. It's called the new covenant here because God confirmed it at the cross—whereas the old covenant had been ratified back at Sinai.

Let's notice the glorious promise of this new covenant, the everlasting covenant:

" 'This is the covenant that *I will* make with the house of Israel: After those days,' says the Lord, '*I will* put My laws in their mind and write them on their hearts; and *I will* be their God, and they shall be My people.' " Hebrews 8:10. Emphasis supplied.

So God said, "*I* will do it. I will put My laws in My believers' minds and hearts." The same Ten Commandments, you see, written on stone under the old covenant are written on human hearts now.

Evidently new-covenant Christians, in appreciation for being saved by grace, will live responsibly, willingly obeying all ten of the commandments.

Let's not confuse this obedience of faith with legalism. You husbands reading this, let me ask you something. When was the last time you bought flowers for your wife? Perhaps when you wounded her feelings by something hasty you said. You tried to regain her favor by bringing home a beautiful red rose. Now, if you had been a really nasty grouch, you probably brought her a dozen long-stemmed roses as a peace offering!

That's called appeasement. But there's another reason you've sometimes bought your wife flowers, a better motivation: appreciation. Remember when you came home with a dozen roses and a big smile on your face—just because you appreciated her and wanted to make her happy—not because you had to earn her favor?

You can see the parallel here. Appreciation for salvation—that's why we keep God's commandments under the new covenant. Not the appeasement, the righteousness by works of the old covenant.

Of course, even though faithful hearts happily honor all God's commandments, we still need mercy to cover our shortcomings. And so the new covenant promise concludes, "I will be merciful to their unrighteousness, and their sins and their lawless deeds I will remember no more." Hebrews 8:12.

Certain things changed when Jesus fulfilled the new covenant.

Christian baptism replaced the act of circumcision, and the Lord's Supper took the place of the Passover feast.

The Passover, you may recall, was one of seven annual sabbaths established at the time of Moses. They were "a shadow of things to come, but the substance is of Christ." Colossians 2:17. After Calvary these yearly sabbaths, along with circumcision, had no further meaning.

The weekly Sabbath, on the other hand, was not a ceremonial shadow introduced by Moses. Rather, it's the eternal memorial established at the creation of the world. It's also our weekly opportunity to celebrate what happened at Calvary. Do you see the difference?

Now, would you picture yourself in the audience at a wedding. As the bride and groom stand expectantly before the altar, you hear the pronouncement, "If anyone can show cause why this marriage should not take place, speak now or forever hold your peace."

There is a deadline, you see. Once husband and wife have sealed wedlock, nothing about their covenant is supposed to be changed.

Did you know the new covenant had a deadline too? Paul said, "If it is confirmed, no one annuls or adds to it." Galatians 3:15.

Once the covenant was confirmed, nothing could be changed.

Baptism came into the covenant before it was sealed at Calvary.

Also the Lord's Supper, which was established the night before Christ's death—just before the deadline. Remember, after the cross, nothing could be added to the covenant or removed from it.

What about the Sabbath? Was it banished from the covenant before Calvary, along with circumcision and the Passover? No, the day after the cross sealed the covenant, Christ honored Sabbath rest. So the sacredness of the seventh day could never be removed from the new covenant.

And what about Sunday keeping? We know from the New Testament that no new day of worship had been added to the covenant before the deadline at Calvary. So Sunday must never be called the Lord's day after the cross. Not by the apostles and not by the Christian church during the centuries since.

Sometimes you will hear that the Sabbath couldn't be kept properly today, because in the time of Moses offenders were punished by stoning. And we don't stone people who break the Sabbath anymore. Therefore the Sabbath must have been abolished. So the reasoning goes.

Well, no true Christian would approve committing adultery, breaking the seventh commandment. Yet in the old days, adulterers were put to death along with those who broke the Sabbath. Today we don't stone sinners for either offense anymore, yet that doesn't make it right to break the seventh commandment. So why should we break the fourth?

The fact is that under Moses, many sins were punishable in ways that don't apply anymore. Those punishments were part of the temporary code of ceremonies not included in the Ten Commandments.

You see, the *Ten Commandments deal with principles, not with punishment*—principles of love.

Consider those commandments, one by one. The first four

explain basic love for God. The last six form the foundation of love for people. And so the New Testament teaches that "love is the fulfillment of the law." Romans 13:10.

God's Word says, "Do we then make void the law through faith? Certainly not! On the contrary, we establish the law." Romans 3:31.

Now, just in case any question remains about the difference between the ceremonial laws, with their circumcision, and the Ten Commandments, let me share one text which should forever clear it up for you. It's 1 Corinthians 7:19:

"Circumcision is nothing and uncircumcision is nothing, but keeping the commandments of God is what matters."

Could we possibly miss the clear distinction here between the eternal Ten Commandments and the temporary ceremonial laws? Circumcision doesn't matter. Keeping the commandments of God does matter—the apostle Paul, inspired by the Holy Spirit, said so.

And remember, it's Sabbath rest in the fourth commandment that gives meaning and purpose to keeping the other nine. *Amid the essential duties outlined in the law, the seventh day offers rest in the work of Christ for us.* We show faith in Jesus, Lord of the Sabbath, by resting as He did on the seventh day.

Some Christians resist Sabbath rest, claiming that they already rest in Christ and therefore don't need God's holy day. The Sabbath is only an institution to them, something unimportant.

Well, remember the hippies back in the sixties? They thought this way about marriage. All you need is love, they insisted. Marriage is only an institution; it's not important.

That's not the way Christians ought to think, is it? Besides, nearly every church has some form of baptism and celebration of the Lord's Supper. These are only symbols, although everyone agrees to their importance. Tell me, if baptism and the Lord's Supper are essential symbols of faith in Christ, why not the Sabbath as well?

Certainly we rest in Christ seven days a week, but the Sabbath is that special day God set aside for us. Think of it this way. Married people are partners seven days a week, yet they need special times set apart from the duties of life. In marriage we are free to choose any time we find convenient for vacations together, but for the Sabbath, the seventh day has been selected by God for us to worship Him.

Because it memorializes creation and salvation, the reasons we worship God, the Sabbath tests our faithfulness to the new covenant. Our willingness to rest in Christ.

But something has gone wrong in Christianity. Something has happened to Sabbath rest. Since the New Testament gives no hint of a change from the seventh to the first day of the week, we must turn to history to find out how, when, and why the change was made. Our next chapter will explore fascinating events that led to an unauthorized change in the Sabbath after the first century.

As you consider the claims of the Sabbath, could it be that you find yourself tempted to resist God's special day? Your hesitancy may find root in the typical human tendency to depend upon your past religious heritage. To say, "If my ancestors worshiped on Sunday and it was all right for them, then it's right for me too."

This may sound fine at first, but think about it. The faith of our grandparents may have been as pure as the snow, and God certainly accepted their sincerity. But today in earth's final hour, with truth unfolding before us, don't we have a responsibility to walk in the light now shining from God's Word? To accept every gem of truth He gives us?

Right now many Christians don't know about Sabbath rest in Jesus. And God understands that. But things are changing fast. Every week 8,000 Christians around the world are keeping their first Sabbath.

Soon God's people everywhere will have entered Sabbath rest. We read in Revelation of the last generation of Christians just before Jesus comes:

"Here is the patience of the saints; here are those who keep the commandments of God and the faith of Jesus." Revelation 14:12.

Faith in Jesus. Keeping God's commandments. They go together, you see, because of Sabbath rest.

What did the assassination of John F. Kennedy do to the Constitution of the United States? Nothing. Those shots fired in Dallas only tightened our determination that our Constitution and all that it stood for would never be lost.

What did the death of Jesus do to change the Sabbath of the new covenant? Nothing but confirm it forever.

What did the cross do to the Ten Commandments? Nothing. Except that the incredible cost of our salvation and the uncompromising loyalty it sparks in our hearts make disobedience unthinkable since the day He died.

The Mystery of Lawlessness

Back in the first century, Christianity was a crime.

Firestorms of persecution swept through the church as Roman emperors massacred thousands of believers.

Those early Christians suffered horrifying deaths for the sake of Jesus. Emperor Nero covered some of them with pitch and burned them at night to light his palace garden. Other believers were slaughtered by sword in Rome's Forum or torn from their families by the teeth of lions.

In this way the devil, working through pagan Rome, determined to destroy Christianity. But it didn't work. Despite fierce opposition the church survived and thrived throughout the empire.

But while standing strong in the face of open opposition, Christianity began to crumble from within. One historian put it this way: "With the malicious irony so often apparent in history, even while they [believers] fought heroically on one front, their position was infiltrated from another."

Christians ready to sacrifice life itself rather than yield their faith in Christ allowed that faith to be corrupted by pagan influences. Lapsing into legalism, they adopted false teachings that suffocated pure gospel truth.

Quietly and gradually the cancer of apostasy spread. Although many believers refused to compromise the gospel, the church in general suffered a serious loss of faith.

Should this surprise us? After all, had not God's people throughout history continually wandered from the covenant?

Indeed, the New Testament had predicted problems within the church. Peter the apostle warned, "There will be false teachers among you, who will secretly bring in destructive heresies. . . . And many will follow their destructive ways." 2 Peter 2:1, 2.

Paul also prophesied that truth would suffer. See Acts 20:29, 30. And he emphasized that this "falling away" would originate within the church. Then he made the stunning revelation: "The mystery of lawlessness is already at work." 2 Thessalonians 2:7.

Already in the first century apostasy had been born.

Let's think about this antichrist power, the "mystery of lawlessness." It doesn't openly attack God's law. Instead, it ingeniously undermines the Ten Commandments.

Mystery of lawlessness—what could this be? What would be a cunning way of working against the law while seeming to build it up? Using even sincere zeal for the law to weaken what it stands for!

That would be mysterious indeed. But it had happened before.

Paul, discussing the spiritual problems of his day, observed that "Israel, pursuing the law of righteousness, has not attained to the law of righteousness. Why? Because they did not seek it by faith, but as it were, by the works of the law." Romans 9:31, 32. Hard to believe, but true: Lawlessness results from attempting to measure up to the requirements of the law. Righteousness by works doesn't work.

Could this be the mystery of lawlessness—undoing the law by overdoing it?

Let me illustrate how this might happen. Imagine a law requiring that you fall asleep by midnight or you would be fined ten thousand dollars. Why, your very anxiety to com-

ply with that commandment would cripple your capacity to
fulfill it.

Let's turn this around now. Suppose the good news came to
you that Jesus Christ fell asleep for you on the cross. He
fulfilled that law on your behalf. With a sigh of relief you
would find rest and soon be off to sleep—fulfilling the law.

Think about it. Turning away from the law to find righteousness in Jesus would seem to make void the law. But "on
the contrary, we establish the law." Romans 3:31.

Fascinating, wouldn't you say?

Paul goes on:

"What shall we say then? That Gentiles, who did not pur-
sue righteousness, have attained to righteousness, even the
righteousness of faith." Romans 9:30.

Gentile believers, by living in Christ without trying to
prove themselves worthy, "attained to righteousness." They
found their lives coming into harmony with the law.

Bible history proves again and again that anxiety toward
achieving perfect obedience leads to the opposite effect, lawlessness. You recall how this happened at Mount Sinai when
the old covenant was broken. The Israelites determined to be
perfect, promising, "*All* that the Lord says we will do." Then
they ended up breaking the law, all because they overlooked
the covenant of grace.

This happened again in the days of Christ. The Pharisees,
extremely zealous to honor God's law, designed a long list of
rules to promote it. But their attempts backfired. Jesus
pointed out, "Thus you have made the commandment of God
of no effect by your tradition." Matthew 15:6.

So now we see the mystery of lawlessness exposed. It's
legalism. Those who center their lives around the law fail
to experience its reality. But when we in sincere faith focus on salvation in Christ, God can fulfill His new-
covenant promise to write the law in our hearts. Paul understood this when he taught, "Sin shall not have domin-

ion over you, for you are not under law but under grace."
Romans 6:14.

Never forget it, friend. Nothing but failure awaits us when
we put ourselves "under the law" by seeking to win accept-
ance with God. But resting in Christ through God's grace
breaks the power of sin. This freedom of forgiveness solves
the mystery of lawlessness. *Here lies the life-changing power
of the new covenant, the result of Sabbath rest.*

Now let's go back to the early church. How did legalism
overcome the good news of salvation in Jesus?

As we already noticed, righteousness by works began un-
dermining Christianity in the days of the apostles. The apostle Paul fought earnestly to rescue the church in Galatia,
which had backslidden from the gospel into legalism. He
warned:

"I do not set aside the grace of God; for if righteousness
comes through the law, then Christ died in vain." Galatians
2:21.

Unfortunately, after the apostles died, legalism ran ram-
pant throughout Christianity. We see this in the life and
teachings of the church fathers.

Take Origen, for example, a vigorous and eloquent defend-
er of Christianity in the third century. Despite his zeal for
Christ, Origen failed to understand that through the
Saviour all believers are equally acceptable in God's sight.
He believed that "perfect" saints, or those nearly so, enjoyed
special access to God. But so-called simple believers had to
content themselves with lesser blessings.

Those who seemed closest to perfection became objects of
veneration. Their prayers were coveted as if they had a
hotline to God because of their superior piety.

Of course, such teaching is foreign to the gospel. All believers share the same perfect record of Jesus Christ. We are
either saved or lost—there are no second-class Christians.
Whatever our level of spiritual growth, we all approach God

through His mercy, not on the basis of our character development. There are no super-saints more acceptable to God than the poorest struggling believer.

Unfortunately, the early Christian church lost sight of the gospel. Rites and ceremonies that Peter and Paul never heard of infiltrated its worship.

Around the third century, penance was introduced for the purpose of helping people take their sins seriously. Rather than rejoicing in the freedom of sins forgiven, some repenting offenders were compelled to stand conspicuously outside the church at meeting times. All this resulted from losing sight of the gospel, the covenant of grace.

In the early fifth century, legalism ascended to new heights when Simeon Stylites climbed to the top of a tall pillar and made his home there. He determined to live quite literally above the world, safe beyond the reach of its comforts and pleasures. For several decades he remained perched on a small platform atop various pillars, exposed and unsheltered from the weather. Finally death gave him rest from his works.

The Christian church venerated Simeon Stylites as a spiritual hero. Upon his death the cities of Antioch and Constantinople competed for the possession of his body. For six centuries ascetics known as pillar saints followed his example by living up on pillars away from the world, pursuing perfection.

Not surprisingly, amid such abounding legalism Sabbath rest fell into disfavor. In its place came the celebration of Sunday, the first day of the week.

How did this come about? For one thing, Christians wanted to distance themselves from anything Jewish. The Jews, you see, had put themselves in the emperor's disfavor by constantly revolting to regain national independence.

And Rome struck back. In 70 A.D. Roman armies stormed Jerusalem. A quarter million Jews were starved, burned, crucified, or otherwise killed. Numerous anti-Jewish riots swept the empire, climaxed by even stiffer penalties for Jews.

Because Christians shared the same heritage as Jews, Romans tended to treat both groups the same. This was unfair. Christians wanted peace with the emperor, rendering to Caesar his due. Yet they suffered just as if they were Jews—on top of the persecution already theirs for Jesus' sake.

After the second destruction of Jerusalem in the year 135, Emperor Hadrian outlawed Jewish worship—particularly their Sabbath keeping. Christians felt compelled to divorce themselves completely from their Hebrew heritage. Gradually they welcomed customs and holy days from the pagan Roman empire, including their weekly day of sun worship. (Our next chapter explores the influence of paganism in establishing the Sunday.)

For several centuries both the Sabbath and Sunday were kept, with the first day of the week gaining more and more prominence. This side-by-side practice continued into the sixth century, with the true Sabbath still holding firm in many areas. But finally the Sunday completely eclipsed the Sabbath throughout the empire, although even then pockets of Sabbathkeepers remained here and there.

The Epistle of Barnabas, written around the year 135, contains the first explicit reference to keeping Sunday. It's interesting to analyze the case presented there for abandoning the Sabbath.

Barnabas argues that Sabbathkeeping is impossible. Impossible until the future life in eternity, because in this world all believers are impure and unholy. Barnabas asks, How can we have rest until God's work within our hearts is complete? But in heaven, he states, "we shall be able to treat it [the Sabbath] as holy, after we have first been made holy ourselves."

How very sad! To Barnabas, holiness meant perfection of

character. But in the New Testament, being a saint means deciding to repent of sin, being set apart to live for God.

Apparently the church was forgetting the gospel through misunderstanding Sabbath rest. You see, we don't rest in Christ because of *our* character development, but rather because of *His* accomplishments.

The apostle Paul taught that God "has made us accepted in the Beloved." Ephesians 1:6. "You are complete in Him." Colossians 2:10. This is the message of the Sabbath.

Had the early Christians retained the pure gospel, they never would have forsaken Sabbath rest. Let's explore this further to learn how the mystery of lawlessness—legalism—assisted Sunday in overtaking the Sabbath.

For Christians in the mid second century, the main reason for keeping Sunday was that this world began to be created on the first day of the week, when God made light.

Before long, Christ's resurrection on Sunday became the dominant rationale for Sunday sacredness. Later on, another reason gained prominence—the fact that the Holy Spirit came to the church on Pentecost Sunday. *The Convert's Catechism of Catholic Doctrine,* 1977 edition, documents this: "The Church substituted Sunday for Saturday, because Christ rose from the dead on a Sunday, and the Holy Ghost descended upon the Apostles on a Sunday."—Page 50.

A favorite verse quoted by church fathers in establishing Sunday sacredness was Malachi 4:2: "But to you who fear My name the Sun of Righteousness shall arise with healing in His wings."

Sunday symbolized spiritual "healing" within the human heart from Jesus, the Sun of righteousness. The process begins when God brings sinners light. Then comes conversion—new life in Christ through His resurrection. Finally the Holy Spirit of Pentecost lives within the believer, restoring the image of God.

All these elements of spiritual renewal exist because of

events that happened on the first day of the week. One author summarized it this way: "The Sunday assembly . . . [is] a celebration of the re-creation of men." —A memorial of God's power to re-create human hearts through the new birth and keep us from sinning. Such is what Sunday represented to the early church in its apostasy.

Well, what could be wrong with that? Remember, we are dealing with a mystery of lawlessness here. Something ingeniously subtle. Something appearing as gospel truth but secretly destroying faith.

Let's go back to Simeon Stylites for a moment, and the problem with Sunday sacredness will come into focus. What was Stylites doing atop that pillar, high in the air? Pursuing sinlessness, spiritual renewal.

As a youth, Stylites had shown unusual religious fervor. While still a shepherd boy in his early teens, he entered a monastery and dedicated himself to imitating the example of Christ. Before long, his quest for Christlikeness took him into absolute solitude. There he passed the entire Lent season without eating or drinking, seeking to subdue the flesh so that the Spirit could rule in his life.

Not satisfied with his spiritual progress, Stylites disciplined himself to stand upright for long periods of time. Finally in the year 423 he mounted a nine-foot pillar in order to escape the world. His pillars got taller and taller as he imagined himself getting closer and closer to God. He died on top of a pillar fifty feet high, never having realized perfection.

Five stories up in the air is pretty high, but not high enough to match the spiritual accomplishments of Jesus. If Simeon Stylites had understood Sabbath rest, he wouldn't have climbed that pillar in the first place. Instead, he would have accepted Christ's perfection as his own accomplishment.

Are you beginning to see what's wrong with Sunday sacredness? It focuses attention on the holiness of the Christian—an imperfect, incomplete ground of hope. The Sabbath, on the other hand, honors the perfect work of Christ done for us. Work pronounced by God to be "very good," done so well that it's finished forever—nothing more can be added to improve it.

Now, certainly Christian growth is important. But we cannot confuse what the Bible calls the "fruit" of the gospel—a changed life—with the gospel itself. The *gospel,* you see, is the doing and dying of Christ. The *fruit* of the gospel is a transformed life because of the indwelling Christ. Do you see the difference?

The Sabbath memorializes the gospel, the *finished* work of Christ in *His* life and death. Sunday was made to memorialize the fruit of the gospel, the *unfinished* work of Christ in *our* lives. The difference between the two is crucial. Only Sabbath rest gives us that blessed assurance that all is well with our souls.

It seems incredible, but it's true just the same—many sincere Christians actually compete against Christ. Seeking to equal His perfect character, they fail to find refuge in Him as their substitute. Yes, they go to Him for strength, but they don't trust His blood to cover their shortcomings.

Because of such legalism, they never find rest. No wonder Simeon Stylites never came down from his pillar—God's work in his life was never finished. So here is the problem with the case for keeping Sunday—it deals with unfinished business. No human being has ever been fully renewed in the image of God, so Sunday offers no basis for rest.

By turning away from Sabbath rest in the completed work of Christ, the church broke the very heart of Christianity. Satan ingeniously diverted attention from the cross, focusing instead on the imperfect spiritual experience of believers.

Do we see the mystery of lawlessness at work here? Remember, Bible history reveals that neglecting Sabbath rest leads to spiritual failure.

At no time was this more evident than on the banks of the Jordan River, when the Old Testament Israelites were poised to enter the Promised Land.

God had brought them through the Red Sea, saving them from slavery. And then He gave them the Sabbath to remind them to look to Him for salvation. See Deuteronomy 5:12, 15. Whatever their weakness and failures, His mighty hand had saved them. And that same power would meet all their needs as long as they trusted Him.

But they forgot the meaning of the Sabbath—they forgot what God had done to save them. Thus they were unprepared for the crisis that came upon them.

Here's what happened: spies who had been sent out to explore the Promised Land returned with bad news. Fierce tribes of giants inhabited Canaan and would have to be conquered.

Confronted with this challenge, the Israelites looked within themselves for evidence that they could overcome. Then, overwhelmed by their inadequacy, they lost heart and demanded to be taken back to Egypt, land of their bondage.

"So we see that they could not enter in because of unbelief." Hebrews 3:19. Forgetting what God had done for their salvation, the Israelites lacked spiritual courage to face the crisis. A whole generation perished in the wilderness because they forgot the Hand that had saved them. Their bleaching bones bore terrible testimony that without resting in Jesus, we have no power to overcome the spiritual challenges that come our way.

After recounting the fatal unbelief of God's people at the Jordan, the book of Hebrews brought a solemn warning to the Jewish Christians of the first century:

"Therefore, since a promise remains of entering His rest,

let us fear lest any of you seem to have come short of it."
Hebrews 4:1.

Of course, all of us come short of perfection. But none of us
had better fall short of entering this gospel rest.

Is this spiritual rest somehow connected with the seventh-
day Sabbath? Indeed so. First the passage mentions how
God's "works were finished from the foundation of the
world." Then it continues, "And God rested on the seventh
day from all His works." Verses 3, 4.

So here we have the seventh-day Sabbath offered as a New
Testament symbol of entering gospel rest. The chapter also
recites the long history of failure on the part of God's Old
Testament people to accept what He had earned for them.
Even after the children of those Israelites who perished in
the wilderness finally entered the Promised Land, their
leader Joshua still could not lead them into Sabbath rest.

Outwardly they kept the Sabbath by avoiding business on
the seventh day. But, like the Pharisees of Christ's day, they
were not true Sabbath keepers. You see, they had never entered the spirit of Sabbath rest. And so we read in verse 9,
"There remains therefore a Sabbath rest for the people of
God." NASB.

Now, what Sabbath rest is this that remains for New Testament believers? Notice the next verse: "He who has entered His rest has himself also ceased from his works as God
did from His."

Well, when did God cease from His works? On the seventh-
day Sabbath, according to verse 4. So this same Sabbath rest
remains for New Testament Christians today.

Does this not mean that the test is our rest in Christ: ceas-
ing from our works on the seventh day, just as God did from
His? This means refraining from works of salvation—we
don't search within ourselves for evidence that God can accept us. Nor do we ask God for help to compete with the character of Christ. Instead, we rest in the finished work of Jesus.

It also means that we rest on the seventh day from all pursuit of secular accomplishment: buying and selling or anything else that pertains to personal gain or business as usual. In fact, we surrender everything that's secular on the seventh day in order to enter God's rest.

Because of all this, the Bible says that the Sabbath is a special sign between God and His people. A sign that He sets us apart from the world to be His children. See Ezekiel 20:12. And He invites us to respond in turn: "Hallow My Sabbaths" (verse 20). That is, "Set the seventh day apart for Me, just as I have set it apart for you. Let's spend that time together each week."

Rearranging our weekend for Sabbath rest may involve some inconvenience or even hardship. Still we are urged, "Let us therefore be diligent to enter that rest, lest anyone fall after the same example of disobedience." Hebrews 4:11.

Any time you take a vacation, you've got to make arrangements with your employer, with your friends and family. Well, the Sabbath is our weekly spiritual vacation. And it takes some effort, some diligence in order to keep that appointment with God.

Yes, we're all busy people. The last thing we may want on Friday afternoon is to set aside our works to rest in Jesus. And that's how the Sabbath tests what is most important to us. Will we consider what God has done for us worth more than what the world offers—more than its business and pleasures, more than news and sports and shopping?

Will we take the day off as a spiritual vacation to be with our loved ones—our families, our fellow brothers and sisters in the Lord? Will we rest from the cares of a busy week to worship, to enjoy nature, perhaps to visit the sick and distressed?

If so, we will find that Sabbath rest in Christ brings strength into our lives. Paul said, "Now may the God of hope fill you with all joy and peace in believing, that you may abound in hope by the power of the Holy Spirit." Romans 15:13.

Power comes through believing! Divine strength excels in human weakness. The mighty, life-changing Spirit of God fills our lives when we enter Sabbath rest in Jesus.

In the gospel of Mark, we find a heartwarming, faith-inspiring story that proves the power of resting in Jesus. The disciples had just returned from a grueling missionary tour. Jesus knew they needed a break, so He said, "Come aside by yourselves to a deserted place and rest a while." Mark 6:31.

Well, it wasn't a deserted place for long. The crowds soon learned of their retreat and flocked to see Jesus. Moved with compassion, our Lord interrupted His time off to minister to their needs. That wonderful day with Jesus passed quickly, as you can imagine. Then late in the afternoon something of a crisis arose.

Hungry children began begging their mothers for food, and there wasn't any. No supermarkets were nearby, even if the disciples had the money to provide for their guests.

To the disciples, only one solution seemed reasonable— sending the people home. Get them away from Jesus so they could go back to the world and have their needs met.

But Christ had a better idea. "You don't have to send them away from Me. There's enough right here for everyone to eat—go ahead and feed them."

The disciples were flabbergasted. They trusted Christ's word all right, but this seemed to be stretching things a bit. All they could scrape together among that whole crowd were five loaves of bread and two fish. How could those thousands of hungry people subsist on that?

But Jesus didn't seem distressed about their lack of resources.

He just said, "What little you may have, entrust it all to Me." And then He did something interesting in the light of what we have been studying. He told the crowd to sit down and rest.

Now, when you are hungry and there's no food around, the last thing you feel like doing is sitting down for rest. You want to rummage around for some food, right?

But the people entered Christ's rest anyway. And Jesus had a surprise for them. You know the thrilling story. He took what little they had, all of it, and blessed it. And miraculously, as they rested on the grass, their need was met. "They all ate and were filled," with baskets of food left over.

What a picture of the Christian life! Often in times of temptation, the enemy suggests that we must leave Jesus in order to have our needs fulfilled. And the mystery of lawlessness insists that we must abandon our rest in Christ by proving ourselves acceptable to God. But our Lord assures us, "I have provided everything you need. Come, for all things are now ready."

Do you see the parallel here, the application for Sabbath rest? Jesus, Lord of the Sabbath, invites us to come apart and be with Him.

To step aside from the world with its busy cares, to come apart from employment that requires breaking the Sabbath, to advance beyond our cherished religious heritage—even if it disappoints friends and family members who may not understand the new light God has shown us in His Word.

Perhaps a barrier like the Jordan River stands between you and entering Sabbath rest. Will you grasp the hand of Jesus and move ahead by faith anyway? The enemy of our souls tempts us to leave the Lord of the Sabbath in order to have our needs met. To break God's holy day by scurrying around getting things done rather than resting in Jesus. But if we will quietly trust in Him, every need will be supplied— with many baskets left over.

Often we hear the words, "Expect a miracle!" Usually the idea is to get what we want from God. But God has a better plan—expect a miracle in getting what He wants. And He wants us to rest in Him.

That's what really makes us happy anyway.

No doubt about it, God will work miracles for you, if that's what it takes, when you step forward in faith to keep the Sabbath. Believe in Him, rest in Him, and He will see you through.

Yes, our Saviour's gracious promise stands forever: "Come to Me, all you who labor and are heavy laden, and I will give you rest."

Centuries Tell Their Story

Hollywood isn't famous for providing spiritual inspiration. But once in a while the smog lifts and a refreshingly different film comes our way. Such as the Oscar winner *Chariots of Fire,* based on the life of Eric Liddell.

Back in 1924, Liddell won fame for his amazing victory at the Olympic Games in Paris. Arms flailing and head thrust back, he stunned the world by winning the 400-meter race.

But Eric Liddell was not a "sportsaholic." Despite his athletic accomplishments, his greatest passion was living for God. He arose early every morning to spend an hour alone with his Lord. Then he forfeited fame and potential fortune to sacrifice his life as a missionary to China.

If you saw *Chariots of Fire,* you remember Liddell's courageous refusal to run races on Sunday. This respect for what he believed to be the Lord's day reflected the faith of many in his native Scotland. As one writer put it, "You can *feel* the Sabbath in the Highlands."

But interestingly, the present day of worship is not the Sabbath that the Highlanders had reverenced until the late Middle Ages. The church in Scotland, founded by the missionary Columba, kept the seventh-day Sabbath, Saturday.

In 1067, when Margaret of England married Malcolm of Scotland, she commented about certain "peculiarities" of the

Scots. For example, she noted, "They work on Sunday, but keep Saturday in a sabbatical manner."

Well, worshiping on the seventh day may have been "peculiar," but it was scriptural. Nevertheless Margaret determined to enforce Sunday observance, already prevalent in England, upon the Celtic church. Even so, on the eve of the Reformation many communities in the Highlands and the Islands continued to keep the seventh day holy.

Faithful believers in other areas honored the Sabbath, centuries after Sunday became the law of the empire. We have record of this in areas as diverse as Egypt, France, Turkey, Palestine, Syria, Italy, France and Yugoslavia. In many places both Sabbath and Sunday were kept.

In the eleventh century Patriarch Caerularius of Constantinople resisted the authority of Rome. Among other reforms he insisted that the church cease its gloomy fasting on the seventh day and honor the Sabbath with joy. But Pope Leo IX declined. Declaring his word to be law for all Christians, in 1054 he excommunicated the entire Eastern Orthodox Church.

Edward Gibbon, in his *Decline and Fall of the Roman Empire,* described how the zeal of ancient Rome faded after Caesar's armies had subdued the world. Later generations, Gibbon wrote, "held in their lifeless hands the riches of their fathers without inheriting their spirit."

It can happen to a nation. Could it happen to a church? Could a church hold in its hands a rich Christian heritage without inheriting the spirit of its founders?

We noticed in our last chapter how apostasy, predicted by the New Testament, overcame the church. Legalistic rites and ceremonies from pagan sun worship became incorporated into Christianity. To help us understand what was happening, it might be helpful here to trace the ancient roots of sun worship.

Adoration of the sun goes all the way back to the time of

Noah. Nimrod, his great-grandson, became a "mighty one on the earth." Genesis 10:8. Beginning with his Tower of Babel, Nimrod's achievements adorn the records and legends of ancient history. But this talented leader was evil. A father of false worship.

False worship also thrived through Ishtar, called the queen of heaven, goddess of love and fertility. Ishtar, according to legend, gave birth to a son, Tammuz, without a father. Here in pagan sun worship centuries before Christ we find a counterfeit of the virgin birth.

Certain of the male gods of fertility became honored as sun gods. They died every winter and had to be resurrected to restore the fertility of plants, animals, and humans.

Ancient Babylon became a center of sun worship. From there, veneration of the sun spread to infect the world. Records and art forms show how each nation reverenced the sun in the customs of its own culture.

But why, we wonder, did they worship the sun? Because the sun brings light, warmth, growth—what we need for life itself. Reigning supreme over nature, the sun is the natural object of worship for those who reject their Creator.

Ceremonies to the sun god were gruesome beyond belief. Babies were burned as living sacrifices, and young women were degraded as sun temple prostitutes. All this to appease the endless appetite of sun deities. If only they had accepted their Creator's gift of salvation!

Time and again the Lord exposed the follies of sun worship. Remember the story of how He rescued His people from Egypt, when He overpowered the sun with three days of darkness? All who turned from the sun god and put the lamb's blood on their doorpost were saved from the death angel. Even so, Israel exported sun idolatry in the Exodus. The golden calf to which they bowed represented Apis, an image closely associated with sun worship.

Through their apostasy and unbelief, an entire generation

of Israelites perished in the wilderness. But their children finally entered the Promised Land of Canaan. Unfortunately, after they died, *their* children reverted to sun worship. Notice:

"When all that generation had been gathered to their fathers, another generation arose after them who did not know the Lord nor the work which He had done for Israel. Then the children of Israel did evil in the sight of the Lord, and served the Baals." Judges 2:10, 11.

How sad that God's people forsook Him for Baal, one of the pagan sun gods. Throughout Old Testament times adoration of the sun corrupted the worship of God in Israel. King Solomon, the very one who built the temple, defiled Jerusalem with paganism. Sun worship flourished. God's people baked cakes to the queen of heaven, according to Jeremiah 7:18. And Ezekiel 8:13-16 records the shocking scene of women reverencing Tammuz in God's temple, with men bowing low before the sun.

Imagine—sun worship ceremonies in God's house! It would happen again in New Testament times, as we shall see. Faithful prophets throughout the Old Testament called Israel away from the sun to their Creator. They pointed to the seventh-day Sabbath, God's weekly reminder of creation. Yet the Hebrews persisted in paganism. At last the Lord gave them up to be captives in Babylon, that ancient center of sun worship.

After returning from captivity God's people finally forsook the follies of their pagan neighbors. But then they went to the other extreme, shunning those around them to avoid contamination. By the time of Christ the Jews had largely quarantined themselves from the Gentiles.

Meanwhile, Babylon fell to the Persians, and sun worship continued to spread. After Alexander the Great conquered the world, the Greeks carried forth their own sophisticated brand of idolatry— including reverence for the sun.

The Romans also venerated the sun in their empire. They named the days of the week according to their heathen religion. On Sunday they reverenced the sun; Monday the moon; Tuesday, Mars; Wednesday, Mercury; Thursday they honored Jupiter. Friday, Venus. Saturday? You guessed it— Saturn. Just as the sun rules over the planets, Sunday rose to honor above other days in the week.

This brings us back up to the first century A.D. First-generation Christians resolutely resisted the influences of pagan worship. But after they died the ceremonies of sun worship gradually became intermingled with Bible truth.

Now why would the church want to mingle paganism with Christianity? We noticed in our last chapter that Christians had determined to escape extra persecution by distancing themselves from anything Jewish. This left them open to influences from pagan society.

With Jerusalem destroyed in A.D. 70, Christians looked to the capital city of the empire as their new church center. Rome's importance to the church increased after the second destruction of Jerusalem in the year 135. When Emperor Hadrian outlawed Jewish Sabbath keeping, Christians felt compelled to completely abandon their Hebrew heritage. They found it all too convenient to borrow customs from the pagan Roman empire.

Have you ever wondered what Easter eggs and bunny rabbits have to do with the resurrection of Christ? Nothing, of course. They were pagan symbols of fertility. The church adopted them to celebrate new life in Jesus. *Grolier's Academic American Encyclopedia,* under the article "Easter," states:

"The name Easter is derived from the pagan spring festival of the Anglo-Saxon goddess Eostre, and many folk customs associated with Easter (for example, Easter eggs) are of pagan origin."

Other heathen feasts besides Easter entered the church.

For centuries pagans celebrated their sun god on December 25. Have you ever heard of that date?

Now, there's nothing morally wrong with exchanging gifts at Christmas—even if it isn't the real date of Christ's birth. Or hiding Easter eggs or putting bunnies in baskets for children. But here's my question. Since our Christian holidays come to us from sun worship, how do we know other areas of our worship, perhaps God's commandments, have not been tampered with too?

Think about it.

Christians seeking relief from persecution welcomed the rituals of sun worship. Of course, nobody suggests they actually worshipped the sun. They were celebrating Christ's birth and resurrection. Even so, they adopted the ceremonies of those who did worship the sun—just as God's Old Testament people did.

Modern scholars recognize these pagan roots in Christianity.

John Henry Newman tells the facts in his book *The Development of Christian Doctrine:*

"The use of temples . . . dedicated to particular saints, . . . incense, lamps, and candles; . . . holy water . . . holydays and seasons . . . are all of pagan origin."—Page 373.

As the church began to reflect its pagan environment, society became comfortable with Christianity. And why not? People could celebrate their heathen holidays in the name of Jesus. But a price had been paid. Pagan tradition had buried Bible truth.

As the ceremonies of sun worship infiltrated Christianity, oppressive legalism replaced the freedom of the gospel. The church enforced fasting on the seventh day, suffocating the joy of Sabbath rest. Other teachings were introduced which denied that the blood of Christ alone qualifies Christians for heaven.

By the fourth century, Christianity so resembled paganism that the emperor found it easy to become a believer. Constantine the Great proclaimed himself a convert in the year 312. Persecution ceased. Outright pagan sacrifices were outlawed, and Christian worship became official. Delighted church leaders pledged to support the new Christian emperor. Hand in hand together, church and state mixed faith in Christ with sun worship rituals.

On March 7, 321, Constantine ordered his empire to regard the "venerable day of the sun." Not the Son of God, but the sun—the day of pagan sun worship. Constantine's use of the old pagan name, "dies Solis" or Sunday, for the weekly Christian festival gives proof that Christianity had indeed become infected with paganism.

Soon Sunday keeping became the law of the land. The writings of the early church fathers bear witness to accelerating apostasy.

Friend, in so serious a matter we must build well. I want you to have the facts for yourself. Yet how shall I know what to select when the historical references documenting these things and the books that contain them would fill a two-ton truck?

Notice this, for example, from *The Paganism in Our Christianity,* a book by Arthur Weigall:

"The Church made a sacred day of Sunday . . . largely because it was the weekly festival of the sun; for it was a definite Christian policy to take over the pagan festivals endeared to the people by tradition, and to give them a Christian significance."

One shudders to believe that such a thing happened in God's church. But the terrible truth is that the Sabbath of the Lord Jesus Christ was sacrificed to the gods of compromise, popularity, paganism, and legalism!

Now consider this compelling conclusion from the respected scholar John A. O'Brien in his current best-seller (1974) *The Faith of Millions:*

"Since Saturday, not Sunday, is specified in the Bible, isn't it curious that non-Catholics who profess to take their religion directly from the Bible and not from the Church, observe Sunday instead of Saturday? . . . That observance remains as a reminder of the Mother Church from which the non-Catholic sects broke away—like a boy running away from home but still carrying in his pocket a picture of his mother or a lock of her hair."

Something to think about, isn't it?

Sunday—not in the Bible. Not a command of Christ. Only a human institution. True, it came into use early in the history of the church. But is it not a tragedy that it came branded with the name of the sun god, tainted with apostasy, a legacy direct from the bosom of paganism?

What a pity that the church received it so willingly, so unquestioningly, so blindly! How could such a thing have happened? How could such a dramatic fracture of truth have gone undetected?

We must remember that before the invention of the printing press the Scriptures were available only to priests, kings, and the very wealthy. Also, the church withheld the Bible from lay members, reserving for its clergy the right to interpret the Scriptures.

All manner of abuses abounded in the church during the dark centuries. Finally reformers such as Martin Luther appeared on the scene and called the church back to the Bible, away from its traditions and back to gospel truth.

In a famous debate with the papal representative Johann Eck, Luther proclaimed that his conscience was captive only to Holy Scripture. *Sola Scriptura* was his slogan—"The Bible and the Bible only." No church tradition could rule his life.

One day, in the heat of battle, Eck decided to call Luther to account for keeping Sunday in place of the Bible Sabbath. Here is his challenge to the reformer:

"Scripture teaches: 'Remember to hallow the Sabbath day; six days shall you labor and do all your work, but the seventh day is the Sabbath day of the Lord your God,' etc. Yet . . . the church has changed the Sabbath into Sunday on its own authority, on which you have no Scripture."

Eck had a point that Luther could not deny. In his battle against church traditions, the reformer had not yet come to grips with the Sabbath question.

The split widened between Rome and the Reformation. Complete severance came after the Council of Trent, where the demands for doctrinal change were officially discussed and finally dismissed.

This historic meeting began in 1545 and continued, on and off, for eighteen years as the debate went back and forth. Finally a speech by the Archbishop of Reggio turned the tide. He argued that tradition must stand above Scripture, because on the authority of tradition alone the church had changed the Sabbath into Sunday.

Here is how Dr. H. J. Holtzmann, in his book *Canon and Tradition,* page 263, summarized the dramatic scene:

"Finally, at the last opening on the eighteenth of January, 1562, all hesitation was set aside: the Archbishop of Reggio made a speech in which he openly declared that tradition stood above Scripture. The authority of the church could therefore not be bound to the authority of the Scriptures, because the church had changed . . . Sabbath into Sunday, not by the command of Christ, but by its own authority."

So what carried the day when all hung in the balance? It was the fact that the church had actually, in effect, changed one of God's commandments, the Sabbath, on the authority of tradition.

Let's look further at what happened to the fourth commandment, which is listed as third in the Catholic catechism. Although some may be surprised at this, the Roman Catholic Church freely informs us of their influence in that change from Sabbath to Sunday. Notice, for example, *The Convert's Catechism of Catholic Doctrine,* 1977 edition, page 50:

"Q. *Which is the Sabbath day?*

"A. Saturday is the Sabbath day.

"Q. *Why do we observe Sunday instead of Saturday?*

"A. We observe Sunday instead of Saturday because the Catholic Church transferred the solemnity from Saturday to Sunday."

Now, Protestants may be more uninformed than Catholics over this revelation. You see, Roman Catholics have taken pride in what they believe to be the authority of the church in interpreting Scripture.

Although I personally cannot accept tradition as having any influence upon belief, I must say that Catholics are at least logical and consistent with their tradition in keeping Sunday.

Perhaps Protestants ought to ask themselves why they keep Sunday, since obviously tradition accounts for its origin. Something to think about, isn't it?

Have we been unwittingly cherishing an institution that is not scriptural at all? Evidently we have.

The story is told of a young Russian czar, many years ago, who enjoyed taking walks in the royal garden. One day he noticed a palace guard nearby standing in all his pomp and ceremony, watching over what appeared to be nothing.

Curious, the czar walked over and asked the young soldier what he was guarding. He didn't know—except that orders called for a sentry at that spot.

The young czar looked up the records. He discovered that at one time the great Catherine had sponsored acres of rare rose gardens. And on that spot a choice and beautiful rosebush had grown. Every week she permitted the peasants to come and view the roses. But she ordered a sentry to stand guard over that particular bush. The order was never rescinded. The rose gardens had long since disappeared.

But a sentry still stood guard—over nothing at all.

Could it be that we have been earnestly and sincerely standing guard over some things that are not sacred at all?

Millions have worshiped on Sunday, considering it a sacred privilege. Like Eric Liddell of *Chariots of Fire,* they have worshiped sincerely, believing it to be the true memorial of our Lord's triumph over death. And God has certainly accepted their sincere devotion.

But is it possible that there may be advanced light for us to follow? Neglected truths from God's Word we need to obey today? The Bible says, "The path of the just is like the shining sun, that shines ever brighter unto the perfect day." Proverbs 4:18.

As the true significance of this matter dawns, what can we do but walk in the light God gives us? Yes, entering Sabbath rest may involve some inconvenience, even pain. But it has always cost something to follow Jesus in history. Why not today?

Christianity has become popular here in North America. Politicians have discovered that connecting themselves with the church helps them get elected. For many of us it's no problem in our community to declare ourselves Christians. Everywhere we see the symbol of the cross proudly displayed.

But tell me. Is the test of true commitment whether we wear a shiny gold cross—or whether we will carry the old rugged cross? Here's what Jesus said: "If anyone desires to come after Me, let him deny himself, and take up his cross, and follow Me. For whoever desires to save his life will lose it, and whoever loses his life for My sake will find it." Matthew 16:24, 25.

Just how do we carry the cross for Christ? For one thing, we accept new truth He shows us in His Word. Truth such as the day God says to remember, the symbol of our salvation in Christ—the only day over which Jesus declared Himself Lord.

Is Jesus worth our complete commitment? Worth the loss of our time, maybe our job, some friends, perhaps even our cherished religious heritage? Think of what it cost Jesus on the cross in order to offer us Sabbath rest. And remember His promise that if we lose our lives for His sake, we will find them.

May I tell you about my father? My dear father, when he passed away, had been a minister for nearly forty years. Before entering the ministry he had been in business in the city of Denver. He was a fine Christian, a Methodist leader of lay groups. One day out on the shipping platform one of his workmen had some minor accident, and he said something a Methodist shouldn't have said. Well, the other workmen gathered around to see if they could help. When they found the accident wasn't too serious they returned to work.

But my father, who had joined them, remained for a moment. He said, "I'm so sorry. I am sure that hurt. But we ought to be a little more careful with our language, don't you think? After all, taking God's name in vain is breaking one of God's commandments.

The man spoke up quickly, "Oh, yes. Thanks for pointing that out. We Christians do get careless." And they prayed together.

My father started back through the passageway to his office, patting himself on the back that he had helped somebody keep one of the commandments. But all at once a voice spoke to him, "But, Vandeman, you're breaking the fourth commandment!"

And it broke his heart. You see, this truth about Sabbath rest had come to my father's attention. For some months he had been battling with conflicting loyalties, trying to make up his mind. He knew what the Word of God said. But there were church ties, his family, his friends, his business. And now he had tried to help somebody else keep the commandments, when he himself was breaking one of them. He hurried back to his office and dropped to his knees and talked to His Lord.

Soon he discovered the delight of entering Sabbath rest. Shortly thereafter he sold his business and went off to a Christian college to prepare for the ministry. He became a power in the pulpit for many years, never regretting taking his stand for truth—even though it had been such a struggle for him to make his decision.

A friend of mine, an evangelist, had just shared this truth about Sabbath rest with his audience. As the last hymn was being sung he slipped out the side door. He wanted to make his way quickly to the front of the church where he could greet the people as they left.

Evidently a gentleman attending that night had slipped out during the closing hymn as well—wanting to be alone, wanting to think and pray. In my friend's hurry to get to the front he almost collided with this tall figure standing thoughtfully in the shadows. He was alone. His eyes were moist. He was deeply moved by what he had heard.

My friend placed a hand on his shoulder, wondering if he could help. The man turned slowly, looked earnestly into his face. "All my life I have prayed for truth. But I never thought to ask God how much it would cost!"

Yes, truth will cost you something—and I don't mean money. It costs our commitment. But think of what it cost Jesus!

In the light of what the Lord of the Sabbath has done to save us, could we *possibly* hold ourselves back from Him?

When No Man Can Buy or Sell

Back in seventeenth-century Virginia, if you skipped Sunday services you were in trouble with the law. You lost your provisions for the following week. That was strike one.

If you missed the second Sunday, you forfeited your allowance and were publicly whipped. Strike two.

The third week, believe it or not, the law called for you to suffer death. Strike three and you're *out*.

America's national pastime is religion, and we are proud of it. But we tend to overlook that our spiritual roots are riddled with intolerance. A century and a half before our Bill of Rights guaranteed religious liberty, unbelief was a crime. Faith was enforced by law.

In these 1980s, many thoughtful observers are concerned that we may be heading back to the days of religious intolerance. Could this really happen in our land of freedom?

Millions of conservative Christians are seeking to save America from immorality through religious legislation. I'm thankful to see this rediscovery of morality, but I'm deeply concerned as well. I'm distressed at the thought of forcing faith on the nation through legislation. You will understand why as we take a look back at colonial history.

Back in the seventeenth century the Puritans came to the New World in search of freedom. They had crossed the Atlantic, escaping persecution by the state church of England—only to create another state church of their own. All citizens were required to support the clergy. Magistrates waged war on heresy. Freedom of conscience suffocated in this Old World-style connection of religion and government.

For example, when William Penn's little band of Quakers sailed past the colony of Massachusetts, they nearly fell prey to a band of Puritan zealots. Listen to this order from Cotton Mather, the famous Puritan clergyman:

"There be now at sea a ship called 'Welcome,' which has on board 100 or more of the heretics and malignants called Quakers. . . . The General Court has given sacred orders to . . . waylay the said 'Welcome' . . . and make captive the said Penn and his ungodly crew, so that the Lord may be glorified and not mocked with the heathen worship of these people. . . . We shall not only do the Lord great good by punishing the wicked, but we shall make great good for His minister and people. Yours in the bowels of Christ, Cotton Mather."

Can you believe it! Thank God, the preacher's persecuting pirates failed. Penn's Quakers landed safely and with their quiet faith settled Pennsylvania.

The Puritans not only tyrannized others, they oppressed their own citizens. They arrested a sea captain and locked him in the stocks after spying him kissing his wife on Sunday. One poor man fell into a pond and skipped Sunday services to dry his suit. They whipped him in the name of Jesus. John Lewis and Sarah Chapman, two lovers, were brought to justice for "sitting together on the Lord's day under an apple tree in Goodman Chapman's orchard."

Incredible legalism! And this in a land of freedom?

When Roger Williams first arrived in the Massachusetts Bay Colony he found a warm welcome. The authorities even invited him to lead Boston's only church. But Williams declined. He could not support the suppression of conscience by government. He knew that most of history's bloody battles have been fought to enforce faith. And all for nothing, since genuine religion cannot be compelled or legislated.

"Magistrates may decide what is due from man to man," Williams said. "But when they attempt to prescribe a man's duties to God, they are out of place." Nothing is more absurd, Williams wrote, than "the setting up of civil power and officers to judge the conviction of men's souls." Williams also insisted that no citizen should be compelled to support the clergy.

"What?" exclaimed the authorities. "Is not the laborer worthy of his hire?" "Yes," Williams replied, "from them that hire him."

Puritan leaders could not tolerate such "new and dangerous opinions." At a formal trial in the year 1635, they condemned Williams and ordered him exiled. And so, banned in Boston, he fled to find refuge with the Indians. "I would rather live with Christian savages," he commented, "than with savage Christians."

Williams purchased property from the Indians and established the first modern government offering full freedom of conscience. His settlement at Providence became the blueprint of the American Bill of Rights a century and a half later.

Williams invited all the persecuted and oppressed to find refuge in Providence, whatever their faith. Even if they had no faith, they were welcome. Unfortunately, leaders of Rhode Island who succeeded Williams lapsed into legalism and intolerance, as we shall see later.

History has shown repeatedly that persecution naturally results when faith becomes law. No wonder our national founders had no use for religion by legislation. And neither does God Himself. Jesus put it plainly: "Render therefore to Caesar the things that are Caesar's, and to God the things that are God's." Matthew 22:21.

So things that belong to Caesar—the government—and the things that belong to God—religious matters—ought to be kept separate. We must not mix government with religion.

The Ten Commandments help us understand the difference between religious laws and civil laws. They consist of two sections: the first four commandments pertain to one's personal relationship with God. Government cannot enforce them. But the last six commandments—"Thou shalt not kill," for example—are civil laws. They regulate society. These commandments the state must uphold by whatever means are necessary to protect life and property.

But when government gets involved with religion, problems arise. Consider the matter of school prayer, for example. I believe our children should lift their hearts in prayer everywhere, including in school. Especially in school! But who should teach our kids to pray? Do we want Catholic prayers? Protestant prayers? Jewish prayers? Does it matter?

Not long ago our California state legislature had a Buddhist chaplain. Would conservative Christians like Buddhist prayers in public schools? Who gets to choose what to pray? And who gets left out? You can see the problem.

Could enforcing school prayer lead to other intrusions into private religion? Perhaps even persecution again? Something to think about carefully.

Now certainly I wish everybody would choose to believe in God and live according to biblical morality. But whose interpretation of the Bible? That is the question. And that's why I believe legislation must never interfere with one's relationship with God. Government should protect religion, not promote it.

Having said that, let me emphasize this: Although I cannot support religious legislation, I do believe government ought to fervently enforce *civil* morality. Many of the concerns of the "New Right" are legitimate and essential. For example, I don't think we have to put up with all this pornography in order to protect the freedoms of the first amendment. And certainly government has the right to protect life, including the heartbeat of an unborn child.

But is the pendulum swinging too far? Are we beginning to violate the sacred circle of the first four commandments, one's personal relationship with God?

Many believe that just so long as government doesn't favor one particular church, all is well. To them, separation of church and state merely forbids a state-sponsored denomination. This may seem reasonable at first—but it's been tried here before with disastrous results.

For example, consider the colony of Maryland. It was founded primarily as a refuge for persecuted Catholics, although Christians of all faiths were welcomed. The Maryland assembly in 1649 proclaimed an Act Concerning Religion, which provided that all who confess Jesus shall be welcomed and tolerated. Yet even this so-called Act of Toleration, as sincere as it was, inspired religious persecution. No liberty was provided for non-Christians. And all who disbelieved a particular doctrine of the Trinity were declared under the death penalty.

Persecution. It naturally results when faith becomes law. Even when nondenominational faith gets enforced.

God Himself will not force faith. So why should we?

Church history from its earliest centuries shows that religious legislation breeds persecution. Back in the year 321 Emperor Constantine declared Sunday a national day of worship. Eventually Christianity became the official state religion by order of Emperor Theodosius. Soon the all-powerful church began persecuting all who resisted her teachings.

Anyone who accepted the Bible as the only rule of faith and who insisted upon Jesus alone as intercessor qualified as a heretic. The burning of heretics began at Orleans, France, in 1022. Persecution intensified during the great Crusades. Then came the infamous Inquisition, when thousands lost their lives for their simple faith in Christ.

How could Christians be so cruel to their brothers and sisters in Christ? Well, church officials believed that killing heretics saved thousands of others from following them into eternal torment. Even the heretics themselves might repent through fear of the flames. At least that's what church fathers hoped for.

Protestants, while rejecting many medieval traditions, held to the concept of state-sponsored religion. They failed to see that religious legislation is legalism. National salvation by works.

Understanding Sabbath rest would have preserved Christians from persecuting, forcing religion upon others. And so they persecuted fellow protestants, and Catholics, too. Force, you see, is quite the opposite of rest. It's the end result of rejecting Sabbath rest.

Throughout Christian history ignorance of Sabbath rest has sparked persecution. You recall that the Pharisees plotted to kill Jesus after a dispute about the Sabbath. Later the Christian church, overcome by legalism, persecuted those who refused to reverence the day of the sun.

As we saw earlier, Sunday persecution happened here in America as well. Even Rhode Island, after Roger Williams left office, passed a Sunday law in 1679 requiring certain acts and forbidding others on the first day of the week. All this for the sake of maintaining morality.

The Bible offers a different solution for the spiritual problems of America—the seventh-day Sabbath rest. Week by week the Sabbath invites our personal expression of faith in God as our Creator and Redeemer. Had the Sabbath always been kept, there would be no atheism. No godless societies.

And Sabbath rest makes us moral without becoming legalistic. The other commandments put us to work. Only the Sabbath offers us rest in Christ. It provides a foundation of faith for the duties to God and neighbor outlined in the other nine commandments.

But many who don't understand Sabbath rest want to

bring back Sunday legislation. They urge Sunday laws in the name of social welfare. Requiring one day off is good for society, good for the family. Even good for saving energy—but don't believe it! Remember that despite good intentions, Sunday laws have always sparked persecution in the past. And the Bible indicates that history will be repeated.

The book of Revelation, describing earth's last crisis, tells us that the final conflict will involve worship. The true worship of God versus worshiping the beast and receiving its mark. Notice Revelation 14:6, 7:

"I saw another angel flying in the midst of heaven, having the everlasting gospel to preach to those who dwell on the earth—to every nation, tribe, tongue, and people—saying with a loud voice, 'Fear God and give glory to Him, for the hour of His judgment has come; and worship Him who made heaven and earth, the sea and springs of water.' "

A message here—the everlasting gospel, with a call for the whole world to worship the Creator. Creation and redemption through the everlasting gospel—the two reasons we worship God. Those twin facts of life memorialized by the seventh-day Sabbath!

Evidently at the end of time the seventh-day Sabbath still stands at the foundation of true worship. And how appropriate—in an age of evolution and secular humanism, the Sabbath every week reminds us that we have a Creator God. And with legalism prospering all around us, the Sabbath invites us to rest in Christ's works for our salvation.

Will the Sabbath indeed serve as a final test of genuine loyalty and obedience? How could it be otherwise, since the Sabbath memorializes the reasons we worship our Lord and Saviour Jesus Christ?

Now for the mark of false worship. Notice that those who receive the mark of the beast "have no rest day or night." Revelation 14:11.

No rest—no Sabbath rest!

But while false worship abounds during earth's final crisis, true Christians everywhere will be keeping God's commandments, honoring Sabbath rest. We see this in the very next verse: "Here is the patience of the saints; here are those who keep the commandments of God and the faith of Jesus." Revelation 14:12.

Faith in Christ and keeping God's commandments—remember, they go together because of Sabbath rest.

The cost of loyalty to God will be high. Earth's powers will declare that "no one may buy or sell except one who has the mark." Revelation 13:17. According to verse 15, there will even be a death decree. Yes, it will require some real sacrifice to remain faithful in such a crisis. But the cost of disobedience to God will be even higher: the terrible seven last plagues of Revelation 16.

No one has the mark of the beast yet. Let me repeat that—no one has the mark yet. God, you see, will not permit anyone to receive that mark until the issues are out in the open. But when the issues are fully explained and all have had opportunity to understand and see the critical and final nature of the matter—then, if we deliberately choose to obey a command of men in place of a command of God, if we yield to coercion and take the easy way out—we will have marked ourselves, by our actions, as no longer loyal to God.

The mark will be there—"in the forehead" if we mentally approve the propaganda of Satan. "In the hand" if we don't approve of it but go along with it anyway, succumbing to the economic boycott. Or because we can't take the ridicule of the crowd. The mark may not be visible to human eyes. But angels will see it—and know where our loyalty lies.

God places His seal only on the forehead, the mind. See Revelation 7:3. Never in the hand, for the Sabbath rest isn't forced. God accepts only willing worship from the heart and mind.

Satan doesn't care how he gets his worship. If he can't win it by choice, he'll take it by force!

Now, I know the matter of God's day of rest may seem trivial. But the Sabbath controversy isn't between one day or another. It involves basic loyalty to God. Let me illustrate.

Remember back in the days of President Eisenhower when Soviet Premier Khrushchev visited America? When he took off his shoe at the United Nations and pounded it on the speaker's platform? Suppose he had demanded we Americans abandon our fourth of July and honor our country on the fifth of July instead? Would Khrushchev have had a right to change our day?

Suppose we had accepted his new day? If so, what would that say about our loyalty to America?

The Sabbath controversy, I say, isn't over a day at all. It's over trust, loyalty, obedience to God. Willingness to enter His rest. The worldwide test is coming soon.

It's difficult to understand how the mark of the beast could be enforced by a supposedly Christian government. But then we remember how Jesus predicted that those who killed His followers would consider themselves servants of God. See John 16:2. It's hard to imagine how Christians in America could ever persecute their fellow believers, but then we remember the Puritans.

No doubt about it, the safety zone between church and state has been shrinking. Not long ago, one Protestant leader declared on national network television that "this notion of the separation of church and state was the figment of some infidel's imagination."

Imagine!

More and more, in harmony with Revelation 13, we see attempts to erode our freedoms. And whenever the power of the state has enforced the goals of the church, personal liberty has been forfeited. Persecution has followed. Remember those old American Sunday laws?

I feel sure of this—when liberty is lost in this country it won't be because Americans have become bigots and tyrants. Rather, I'm convinced our freedoms will be voted away, legislated away, amended away by well-meaning conservatives who do not realize what they are doing. They will sacrifice our liberties trying to solve our national problems. In a backlash against decades of permissiveness, in a reaction against shrinking morality, in the belief that returning to lost values is our only hope. They hope to regain divine favor—and discover too late they have forged shackles for the soul.

All this might happen during a national crisis. History shows that people in trouble willingly trade off liberty for security.

Remember how the Nazis gained control over Germany? And look at the fundamentalism in Iran today. Even here in this country, we could easily exchange some of our freedoms for the sake of economic and military security. And as a result, patriots will persecute in the name of God and country.

Racing toward the crisis hour, we cannot ignore or escape the issues at stake. And our decision must be our own. Satan would like to force his way in. Sometimes even loved ones want to enter—loved ones who do not understand. But God Himself won't violate our freedom to choose. He stands at the door of our hearts and knocks. He waits for us to accept His love.

And the honest in heart all over the world will respond to God's call, even at the threat of losing their lives. After all, Jesus promised, "If you lose your life for My sake, you will save it."

I think of that winter night when the Roman legion was encamped by a lake in Armenia. There are several versions of the story. But evidently forty soldiers had refused to recant their faith. And they were sentenced to die out on the frozen lake.

Banded together in the numbing cold, they began to sing.

The stern, pagan commander, on watch from his comfortable tent, heard the words: "Forty wrestlers, wrestling for Thee, O Christ, claim for Thee the victory and ask from Thee the crown."

Strangely moved, that hardened general, so used to cursing and frantic pleas for mercy, listened intently. These were men of his own company, men who had angered the authorities by their faith. These were his forty heroes, distinguished soldiers. Must they die?

He moved out into the cold, gathered driftwood from the shore, and built a huge fire with flames leaping high into the night.

Perhaps this would lead them to renounce their faith and save themselves. But no. Again the sound of the refrain met his ears, weaker now:

"Forty wrestlers, wrestling for Thee, O Christ . . ."

Then suddenly the song changed: "Thirty-nine wrestlers, wrestling for Thee, O Christ . . ."

And all at once, as the song still floated in across the ice, one of the prisoners climbed up the bank and dropped by the fire, a shivering mass. The song of the forty was no more. One of the heroes had disavowed his faith.

On the shore, clearly outlined against the fire, stood the commander. Strange thoughts surged in his heart. Suddenly he took one brief look at the pitiful traitor before him and threw off his cloak. Before his soldiers could stop him, he raced down the bank and across the ice to the freezing prisoners, casting back the words, "As I live, I'll have your place."

In a few moments the song, with a fresh note of triumph, was wafted again to the soldiers who had gathered, fearful and awestruck, on the silent shore: "Forty wrestlers, wrestling for Thee, O Christ, claim for Thee the victory and ask from Thee the crown!"

Tyranny of the Crowd

Come with me to the Alps of northern Italy—a panorama of breathtaking beauty. Here we find snow-capped peaks in their towering majesty. Rich green valleys watered by clear-running streams. Rolling meadows carpeted with fragrant wildflowers. Hillside orchards ripening with luscious fruit.

This is God's country, almost heaven on earth. Here, throughout the dark centuries of apostasy, the Waldenses preserved the ancient faith of the apostles. Faith which had suffered neglect and abuse by the established church.

I think of Henri Arnaud, one of the leaders of the Waldenses.

One spring day, high on Sugar Loaf Mountain, his group watched as soldiers below prepared to attack them. They listened as Colonel de Parat invited villagers there to a public hanging the next day: "Come and see the end of the Waldenses!"

But God had other plans for His people. High atop the peak, Henri Arnaud opened his Bible and read to his company from Psalm 124:

"If it had not been the Lord who was on our side, when men rose up against us, then they would have swallowed us alive." Verses 2, 3.

That night, under the cover of dense fog and darkness, the Waldenses slipped silently away over a mountain pass to safety. When the soldiers closed in for the kill the next day, they found only empty barracks. Bitterly frustrated, the soldiers complained, "Heaven seems to take special interest in preserving these people!"

But countless Waldenses did die for their faith. One sad day a group of them were worshiping in their secret cave, called *Chiesa de la Tanna*—"Church of the Earth." Suddenly soldiers appeared and built a fire at the mouth of the cave. As the oxygen in their cave was consumed, the Waldenses sang praises to God until breath was gone, glad to give their lives rather than renounce their faith.

No one knows how many faithful believers spilled their blood during the long exile of the church in the wilderness. Not until eternity will we know the price they paid for following conscience.

At this point in the twentieth century, Americans don't suffer open persecution for worshiping God according to truth. That time will come soon enough, according to the prophecies of Revelation. But meanwhile, like the Waldenses, are we willing to be different for Jesus' sake? Or are we unwitting slaves to popular opinion—the tyranny of the crowd?

Too many of us follow truth only if it fits in with community custom, only if it makes no demands on us. But it will cost something to follow Jesus. The price of being different.

Why this strange urge to be like everyone else, to do what everybody else is doing? Where is the creative nonconformity that produced the heroes and the martyrs of the past? The excitement of taking a stand! We seem to be hypnotized with the childhood game of follow-the-leader.

Margaret Applegarth has written a delightful book called *Men as Trees Walking*. In it she tells the story, true but almost unbelievable, of Jean Henri Fabre and his study of the processionary caterpillar.

It seems that this caterpillar wanders about aimlessly,

pursued by many followers who move when he moves, stop when he stops, and eat when he eats. Pine needles are their principal source of food.

One day Fabre tried an experiment. He filled a flowerpot with pine needles, which they love, and then lined up the caterpillars in a solid ring around the rim of the pot. Sure enough, they began to move slowly around and around the rim, each following the one ahead. And yes, you've guessed it. They continued this senseless revolving for seven days, never once stopping for food—until one by one they began to collapse. And the author remarks significantly that the woods are full of processionary caterpillars—uncannily like people you and I know.

Following the crowd—even if it takes us round and round, arriving nowhere, missing the rewards of life. Round and round the flowerpots of conformity—until we collapse.

And we don't know why!

It isn't always safe to follow the crowd. To have followed the public mood in Christ's day would have been to reject Him. Listen to the report of the officers sent out to arrest Jesus, but who returned without Him. "The officers answered, 'No man ever spoke like this Man!' Then the Pharisees answered them, 'Are you also deceived? Have any of the rulers or the Pharisees believed in Him?' " John 7:46-48.

This was the question that derailed so many from following Jesus. They had been deeply moved by Christ's message. But when reminded that the religious leaders had rejected Him, they surrendered conscience and forfeited faith. Do we have that problem today?

Truth still burns its conviction into human hearts. It may be startling truth. It may seem strange to modern ears. It may concern the day God says to remember. And there are those who ask, "Have the great religious leaders of our day accepted it? Has it been received into the mainstream of religious thought?"

But the majority, it seems, has seldom been right. The majority, except for eight people, rejected truth in the days of Noah and perished in the catastrophe that public opinion said could never happen.

Truth in Elijah's day was so unpopular that he complained to God that he alone was left. And the 7,000 loyal hearts of whom he was reminded were a pitifully small minority. It took courage for them to be different.

And it took courage for Noah to stand alone against a scoffing world. It took courage for Elijah to stand alone on Carmel against those who sought his life. It took courage for Martin Luther to stand alone before the council that called him to account and demanded that he recant. But his words rang clear and strong and fearless into the ears of his enemies, "I cannot and I will not retract. . . . Here I stand, I can do no other!"

It will take the same courage today, in the closing hours of earth's history. The courage to be different. Courage to be set apart for God.

Truth is a test of our commitment. Sabbath rest in Jesus measures our willingness to be different—if that's what it takes to be faithful to God. You might say the Sabbath keeps us from becoming processionary caterpillars! Not that the seventh day has any value in itself. It's rather what the day represents. Let me illustrate what I mean.

Many years ago I was seated in the dining car on a train. The back of the menu caught my attention with an engraving of the Stars and Stripes in full color. As a loyal American, you can imagine my surprise and my perplexity as beneath the flag I read these words:

"Just an ordinary piece of cloth. That's all it is. You can count the threads in it, and it's not different from any other piece of cloth."

My patriotism would have rebelled if I had not read on: "But then a little breeze comes along, and it stirs and comes to life and flutters and snaps in the wind—all red and white and blue—and then you realize that no other piece of cloth could be just like it."

Yes, that flag is just a piece of cloth until we breathe life into it. Until we make it stand for everything we believe in.

I might take an ordinary piece of red cloth. It's not worth much by itself. But add some white cloth and some blue cloth and sew them all together into the Tricolor of France. Frenchmen will die for their flag! Sew them together into the Union Jack, and Britishers will lay down their lives for it. And if you sew those same ordinary pieces of cloth into the Stars and Stripes, Americans will die for it!

Just so, God took an ordinary day. But then He set it apart from other days of the week and made the Sabbath. He made it represent the greatest things He's done for us in making us and saving us.

You recall that creation and salvation are the two main reasons given in God's Word for worshiping Him. And since the Sabbath is God's appointed memorial of these twin facts of life, you can see now why the seventh day is important to you. How Sabbath rest in Jesus is basic to your relationship with Him.

The deeper you study into this thing, I believe the greater will be your conviction that Sabbath rest is your next step with Jesus. And the sooner you take that step, the sooner you will experience the excitement of stepping away from the crowd and taking a bold stand for your Saviour and Lord.

You may have heard of the Flat Earth Society. They have convinced themselves that our world is not shaped like a ball but rather like a platter. You can even hear them arguing on radio talk shows. When shown photographs that prove the earth is round, they explain, "It's round like a coin but also *flat* like a coin."

Well, the Flat Earth Society had some fancy explaining

to do after that remarkable little plane the *Voyager* flew nonstop around the world. But they somehow managed to hold on to their preconceived beliefs. They seem to find comfort believing only what their beloved ancestors taught centuries ago. They refuse to accept the unfolding evidence of science.

I wonder if some Christians today belong to a religious Flat Earth Society. Convinced by the creeds of their ancestors, they are reluctant to move ahead with the unfolding evidence of Scripture. How much today we need to rekindle the spirit of the reformers! The spirit of adventure, the willingness to accept new truth from God's Word.

We opened this chapter with the inspiring story of the Waldenses and how they stood firmly for God amid terrible persecution. Unfortunately, there is a sad postscript to that story I must share with you.

Not many years ago, near the little Waldensian village of Torre Pellice, a group of Christian youth gathered around their campfire to sing and pray. Visitors from the surrounding valleys and mountains had drifted into the village, and now they approached the campfire with curiosity. Who were these young people? They heard them praying. They heard them singing about the second coming of Jesus, in which their own fathers had once so ardently believed. It brought a strange nostalgia for their own past.

On this night, after the singing and praying was over, one of the Waldensian elders stepped from the shadows into the light of the campfire and spoke thoughtfully to my friend who was in charge, "You must carry on!"

And then he unburdened his heart: "We, the Waldensian people, have a great heritage behind us. We are proud of the history of our people as they have fought to preserve the light of truth high upon these mountaintops and up and down these valleys. This is our home. Here we have the great monuments of our faith. . . . Of all this we are proud."

And then this Waldensian elder, a layman in the church, said with conviction, "This is our great heritage of the past, but we really do not have any future. We have given up many of the teachings in which we once believed. From all that I can observe, from what I have heard about your people, *you* must now carry on!"

What a tragedy it is to stagnate, to fall asleep, or to simply stand still when we might be moving into a future far brighter than the past! What a tragedy to abandon our beliefs—or water them down until we have compromised the ancient faith!

Such is the haunting story of the Waldenses! What a warning to us today.

From old England comes the account of a little boy named Bron who went to church for the first time with his governess. The minister climbed high into the pulpit and then told a piece of terrible news. He told how an innocent Man had been nailed to a cross and left to die.

How terrible, the lad thought! How wrong! Surely the people would do something about it. But he looked about him, and no one seemed concerned. They must be waiting for church to be over, he decided. Then surely they would do something to right this horrible deed.

He walked out of the church trembling with emotion, waiting to see what the crowd would do. But his governess only said, "Bron, don't take it to heart—someone will think you are odd!"

Odd—to be upset, disturbed by injustice? Odd—to be awake to so tragic a recital? Odd—to care, and want desperately to do something about it?

Oh, God, make us odd—if that is what it takes!

I ask you, Do you want to come out from the crowd? Do you want to be released from its spell? Do you want the courage to stand alone?

Heaven will give it. The incomparable power of the cross of

Calvary will be yours as you take your next step with Jesus.

A closing thought from the author—

Dear Friend:

And now a personal word. If the message of this book were a political lecture, if these were ordinary times, you might appreciate what you have read and merely remark, "Well, that's interesting. This has added to my store of information." And all would be well.

However, I earnestly believe that the issues we have discussed bring us face to face with the most important decision we can make, that of placing ourselves on God's side. It's not enough to acknowledge truth. One must act upon it. Just as it's not enough to applaud the lifeboat. One must get into it.

I have made my decision. I have found a group of sincere, earnest Christians who are willing to worship Christ as Creator in this careless age, who are willing to honor the day God says to remember. They are known as Seventh-day Adventists. Their churches are open every Sabbath.

This coming Saturday, more than five million Adventists around the world will be keeping their weekly appointment with Jesus. Eight thousand will be celebrating their first Sabbath. I invite you, urgently, to visit with them. You will be delighted that you did.

Just contact the nearest Seventh-day Adventist church. Let the pastor know of your desire to enter Sabbath rest. Or write to me about your decision, in care of It Is Written, Box 0, Thousand Oaks, California 91320.

You will find it a thrilling, rewarding experience to worship on the day God says to remember!

Sincerely yours in Jesus,

George E. Vandeman